HOME SCHOOLING

Answers to Questions Parents Most Often Ask

Written by Deborah McIntire and Robert Windham

CTP Creative Teaching Press, Cypress, CA 90630

Acknowledgments

A special thanks to Margaret, Emily, Amy, Larry, and Zachary.

In addition, a special thank you to:

Debby La Roy, President
Canadian Home Educators' Association
1994–

Sheree Dennee, Principal
Community Home Education Program
Orange County, California

Robert G. McLure, Principal
Regional Correspondence School
Nelson, British Columbia

Library of Congress Cataloging-in-Publication Data
   McIntire, Deborah 1953–
   Home schooling: answers to questions parents most often ask /
written by Deborah McIntire and Robert Windham
   p. cm.
   Includes bibliographical references
   ISBN 0-916119-84-X
   1. Home Schooling–Handbooks, manuals, etc.
   I. Windham, Robert, 1951– .   II. Title.
LC40.M147   1995
649'.68–dc20   95-13223
                                              CIP

Home Schooling: Answers to Questions Parents Most Often Ask
Copyright © 1995 Creative Teaching Press, Inc.
All rights reserved. However, individual purchaser may reproduce
designated forms in this book for personal use.
Written by Deborah McIntire and Robert Windham
Cover photography by Michael Jarrett
Illustrations by Catherine Yuh
Project Director: Luella Connelly
Editor: June Hetzel
Art Director: Tom Cochrane
Book Design: Jerome Stine

ISBN: 0-916119-84-X
EAN: 9 7780916 119843 9000
CTP: 3340

FIRST PUBLISHED JUNE 1995 IN THE UNITED STATED OF AMERICA BY:
CREATIVE TEACHING PRESS, INC.
P.O. BOX 6017, CYPRESS, CA 90630-0017

LETTER FROM THE AUTHORS

Dear Parent,

During the course of the last ten years, it has been our great pleasure and delight to work closely with over five hundred home-school children and their parents in the role of supervising teacher. We have worked in the private sector and under the direction of the Orange County Department of Education in California. We have had the wonderful opportunity of sharing home educators' struggles, frustrations, joys, and triumphs. This experience has had a positive and profound effect on our personal and professional lives. It has been a continuous revelation as we have witnessed time and again the power of personalized instruction, the innate intelligence of children, and the intuitive wisdom of parents.

Over the years we have noticed a commonality of questions and concerns affecting our home-schooling families. We wrote this book to address these recurring issues. The chapters are organized around the most commonly asked questions. Our responses are drawn from the experience of home-schooling parents themselves and our professional experience and observations as well as from pertinent research findings.

If you are a prospective home-schooling parent, we hope this book will assist you in determining whether home schooling is right for you and your family. If you are a novice home-schooling parent, we provide you with information on instructional approaches and curriculum, record keeping procedures, organizational tools, and practical tips. If you are an experienced home-schooling parent, it is our desire to reinforce and revitalize your home-schooling commitment.

Sincerely,

Robert Windham
Deborah McIntire

CHAPTER 5   EVALUATION

CHAPTER 6   FINDING THE BALANCE

CHAPTER 7   RESOURCES

The Wevodau Family

Fred, Linda

Amy (18)

Sara (16)

Hannah (13)

Daniel (9)

—13 Years

Home Schooling

I home schooled our oldest for first through fourth grades. At the luncheon last year where she was one of six honored graduating seniors, she introduced me as her first teacher. She said those early years developed a confidence in herself, in me, and in our relationship that has stood the test of time. —Linda Wevodau, home-school mom

Initial Questions

- Why would I want to teach my children at home?

- How will my children benefit from home education?

- What about socialization?

- What if I have never taught before?

- What if I do not have family support?

- What are the characteristics of a successful home-school parent?

- What financial aspects must be considered?

Why would I want to teach my children at home?

Home-school parents express a variety of reasons for educating their children at home, including individualization, family time, and strong academic, moral, and religious foundations.

INDIVIDUALIZATION

Home education is a wonderful opportunity to tailor your children's instructional program to their specific learning needs, abilities, and rates. Individualization allows children to work to their potential and increases the probability of educational success and personal satisfaction derived from the learning experience. Home education alleviates parents' concerns that their children are "falling between the cracks" or are not working to their potential in their current schooling situation.

TIME TOGETHER

Some parents home educate because they desire additional time with their children. It has to do with sentiments of "children are only young once" and "they're gone before you know it." These parents want to spend as much time as possible with their children. Sometimes parents of older children just want to get "reacquainted" and/or strengthen family bonds as the challenging age of adolescence approaches. Families spend time together to learn about each other as well as to learn

Home schooling gives me the freedom to teach at my child's own pace.

—Elizabeth Caro, 3 years home-school parent

about facts and ideas. Parents find great satisfaction and pleasure in learning more about their children while helping their children learn more about themselves and the world around them.

Families in rural settings and families with special medical needs also enjoy the additional time home schooling affords them. Families in rural situations find that home schooling can minimize hours of commuting. Families of children who have special health problems find that some medical conditions can be more easily managed at home.

A STRONG ACADEMIC FOUNDATION

Many parents home school because they feel their children need to become more secure and confident in their academic abilities and skills. For some children this strong academic foundation may be more easily realized in the intimate setting of the home where a child receives individualized or small-group instruction. In order to do this, home-school parents may postpone their children's entry into formal schooling for a year, while other parents may choose to home school for all the primary or elementary grades. Still others will home school up to and through the high school level.

A STRONG MORAL OR RELIGIOUS FOUNDATION

Many parents desire strong religious training and values training for their children. Home schooling offers an extended time and place to achieve this objective. It also offers parents the opportunity to help children integrate religious values with curriculum content. For many parents, religious training and values training are key reasons for why they home school.

EDUCATIONAL PHILOSOPHY

Many parents home school to provide their children with an education aligned with their personal educational philosophy. It may be that their child is developing at a quicker or slower pace than his or her peers and that they wish to provide a more personalized instructional setting. Other parents may want to take a more interest-based approach to home education, using their children's questions to plan the lessons for their curriculum. Other home-school parents may disagree with the basic processes and goals of contemporary schooling which might involve curricular, testing, or social concerns. Whatever the philosophical concern, parents who home school feel this decision enables them to provide an education aligned with their philosophy.

Home schooling is much harder than I thought it would be—and much more rewarding! The bond between parents and children cannot be duplicated by any outside school.

—Holly Preston, 2 years home-school parent

How will my children benefit from home education?

Home education provides a unique opportunity for young learners. The most commonly cited benefits include individualized education, interest-based education, and pacing.

INDIVIDUALIZED EDUCATION

The goal of individualized instruction can be realized through home education. Parents can decide their children's educational needs and then provide for those needs. The ongoing, self-adjusting feedback system that has been established from birth by loving, caring parents now becomes part of the child's educational environment. The parent, as teacher, can immediately tell if his or her child is grasping a particular idea or skill. If not, needed adjustments in materials and presentation can be made. In essence, home schooling is a tutorial situation tailored to meet a child's specific needs and learning styles.

One thing I really like about home schooling is that I can learn at my own speed.

—Hannah Wevodau, age 13

Hannah Wevodau, age 13 writes about her own home-school experience—*One thing I really like about home schooling is that I can learn at my own speed. I used to be slow in reading, but instead of being in school where I would be in an easier class when my thinking skills were at normal level, my mom just home schooled me. She read me my history and science, and after a while I was at the normal level, even higher. In math, where I am really strong, I can go ahead up to a level that challenges me.*

Linda Wevodau, Hannah's mother, writes about Hannah—*Our third child had speech difficulties and was an extremely late reader. With no peer comparisons academically, she developed in her own time and has self-confidence in her abilities now. She was able to keep up with her grade level and interests even though she could not read much of the material in those early years. I believe her blossoming and the role I've played with her may become the single most valuable contribution of home schooling to our family.*

INTEREST-BASED EDUCATION

Your children can pursue their interests. Children as well as adults learn more quickly, with less effort, and with greater retention when they are interested in what they are doing (Moore, Raymond and Dorothy Moore. *The Successful Home-School Family Handbook*. Nelson, 1994, pg. 2). Children's minds are eager to be challenged. As children explore their interests, learning becomes meaningful

Children as well as adults learn more quickly, with less effort, and with greater retention when they are interested in what they are doing.

and enjoyable. For example, ten-year-old Samantha is highly gifted and talented in the area of music. She studies at home and condenses most of her academic studies into the morning hours. Her afternoon hours are reserved for studying piano, violin, and voice. She also spends several hours a week working on her own compositions. With a traditional school schedule, it would be almost impossible for her to pursue her musical interests to this extent. Home education provides the time and opportunity to acknowledge and tap into her interests and hobbies. When interest and pleasure are present, learning is inevitable.

PACING

As a home educator, you need not feel the pressure of following the exact time line of a particular textbook. Your children can work at their own rates. For example, Jason, a fifth grader, understood three-digit multiplication and worked through this section of his math book twice as fast as the textbook suggested. When Jason encountered the fraction unit, he required an extra two weeks to understand the concepts introduced.

As a home-school parent, you have the luxury of allocating as much or as little time to instruction in a particular area as you deem appropriate. Trust your instincts. You will quickly learn what does or doesn't work for your children.

When they are ready, move on. If they are not ready, and you believe the idea or skill is important, then present the information again in a different format. Or, you may decide the information is not appropriate just yet and choose to move on to something else. When a child is allowed to progress at his or her pace, learning becomes easier. The experience is more pleasurable and rewarding for both teacher and student.

Some children, because of their particular needs, may have difficulty acquiring basic skills. Compensation skills may need to be taught. If this is the case, then seek help. Ask advice from several sources such as trusted friends, relatives, or educators. Your concern may be short-term. It may be that your child is developing slowly right now but will catch up academically in no time. However, if lingering doubts haunt you, trust those instincts and seek professional help. It may be that your child has a special learning need that should be addressed immediately to save your family hours and even years of anguish in the future.

REAL-WORLD EDUCATION

Children educated at home have additional opportunities to observe parents in real-life situations. Children prepare for the real world by actually living and moving in that world as they go to the grocery store, post office, and toy store. Watching mature adults interact with people of all ages and occupations provides a strong model for helping a child gain maturity and social skills naturally.

Many parents also enjoy the additional time and flexibility home school provides to teach life skills such as cooking, sewing, gardening, general home repair, car repair, budgeting, and bookkeeping. Parents also find home education affords their children ample time on the computer to develop computer literacy—an important skill that will serve their child well in the future.

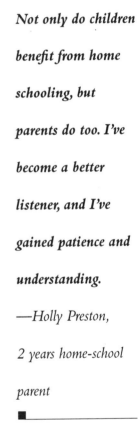

Not only do children benefit from home schooling, but parents do too. I've become a better listener, and I've gained patience and understanding.
—Holly Preston, 2 years home-school parent

What about socialization?

The family unit has been the primary force for socialization until recent history. Basic social skills and attitudes in a cross-generational setting are developed at home, primarily during the first six years of life.

"What about socialization?" is probably the question most asked of home educators. It is also the most frequently stated objection or concern of friends and relatives regarding home schooling. It is important to remember that socialization begins at home.

SOCIALIZATION BEGINS AT HOME

Children learn how to interact and the value of interacting from their parents. Parents model social skills when they interact with each other, family, friends, and neighbors. Home education can be an extended opportunity for this natural process of socialization to continue.

SOCIALIZATION OPPORTUNITIES

Socialization is an important part of *every* child's education. Home-schooled children have the opportunity to develop their communication skills within a broad social context. Home-educated children can socialize with peers after school and on weekends, and they can socialize with adults at home and in the community. They can sign up for dance classes, theater groups, music lessons, church choirs, and sports teams. They should also be encouraged to attend classes and field trips sponsored by support groups and public or private school independent study programs. The average home-schooled child attends more educational field trips during the year than most children who attend school. Therefore, they have the opportunity to observe, move about, and interact within a broad social context.

One of the benefits that many families appreciate about the home-school setting is that for a period of time in their child's life, the parent can be selective about the peer group in which their child interacts. Though no child or situation is perfect, many parents hope that by the time the child enters or returns to the traditional school setting, his or her values will be strong enough to withstand peer influence that may be contrary to family values and productive citizenship.

APPROPRIATE SOCIALIZATION

There is appropriate (positive) socialization and inappropriate (negative) socialization. Many parents decide to home educate because of the *type* of socialization they feel occurs at their particular local school. These parents want to postpone negative social lessons that might occur in the larger school setting which could involve conformity, ridicule, competition, popularity contests, teasing, bullying, and defiant behavior. Of course, these situations can and will occur in the neighborhood just as well, but then a parent is more readily available to counsel and guide.

Important positive social skills such as kindness, patience, respect, understanding, and generosity, as well as their underlying moral values can be taught at school or at home. Home educators feel these positive skills are more easily modeled and taught in the closely supervised context of the home.

Sending a child to school does not insure proper social development and neither does home schooling your child. Whether you choose to educate your child at home or at your local public or private school, it is imperative to be actively involved in influencing the social context in which your child lives. Home schooling provides parents a great opportunity to influence their child's social development.

There are lots of field trips and workshops available for home-school kids and parents so I don't have to worry about my child missing out on social interaction with other children.
—Elizabeth Caro, 3 years home-school parent

DEPENDENCE VERSUS INDEPENDENCE

Sometimes the opinion is expressed that, in addition to developing social skills, sending a child to school fosters independence. That's true, but independence from what or whom? Parents sometimes find that children attending school *are* more independent—*of their parents and their parents' values* while becoming more *peer-dependent.* Cornell University researchers found that children who spend more time with peers than with their parents become peer-dependent. The researchers concluded that the factors important to positive socialization such as self-worth, optimism, respect for parents, and trust in peers were diminished in peer-dependent children (Bronfenbrenner, Urie. *Two Worlds of Childhood: U.S. and U.S.S.R.* Simon and Schuster, 1970, pp. 97-101).

Home educators want children who can make their own decisions based on a foundation of family values and morals. They want peer-independent children. They feel this is more easily accomplished when children spend more time with their family and less time with peer groups.

> *To home educators, the real world is the daily interaction which occurs within the family, neighborhood, and community.*

REAL-WORLD EDUCATION

Related to the issue of socialization is the attitude that children should be in school to learn how to deal with the real world. In the eyes of home educators, placing their children in a school does not necessarily teach them about the real world. To home educators, the real world is the daily interaction which occurs within the family, neighborhood, and community. It should be noted, however, that group work and group interaction may be a large part of a child's future career. A discerning family will look for opportunities to accommodate group experiences.

RESEARCH ON SOCIALIZATION

Finally, the concern over whether home education has a negative impact on a child's social development is based more on attitude and bias than on experience. Studies indicate that home-educated children score higher on measures of self-esteem (Ray, Brian D. *Home School Researcher,* Vol. 7, No. 1, March 1991).

John Taylor Gatto, the outspoken 1991 New York State Teacher of the Year, said that home-educated children can be socially five to ten years ahead of their classroom counterparts (Gatto, John Taylor. *Dumbing Us Down: The Hidden Curriculum of Compulsory Schooling.* New Society Publisher, 1992). Our experience supervising home-school families has been that most home-school children are polite, friendly, and at ease with people of all ages. Their daily experiences include a wider variety of people so they are less age-restricted. They are equally comfortable with younger children, peers, and adults.

So what about socialization? Does educating children at home hinder or harm their social development? Experience and research indicate that for most home-schooled children, the home-school experience is a catalyst for rapid and beneficial social growth. A key to remember is that each child is an individual with individual needs. Home schooling is not for everyone. Some children thrive in the traditional school setting while others flounder. Evaluate your situation and do what you feel is best for *your* child.

Some children thrive in the traditional school setting while others flounder. Evaluate your situation and do what you feel is best for your child.

What if I have never taught before?

Many parents who wish to home school their children, question whether or not they are qualified to take on such an enormous task. It is important to remember that, as a parent, you already are a teacher.

PARENTS ARE TEACHERS

You are your child's first teacher. You have taught your child since birth, from the simple task of recognizing common objects to the complexities of using spoken language. You have played a part, whether large or small, in your child's acquisition and mastery of thousands of skills and ideas. You have helped your child understand the world. Even if he or she enters a formal school setting, your role as teacher is not over. His or her moral, social, and intellectual development is an ongoing process that you will address until, and possibly into, adulthood. Parents spend hours weekly helping their child understand and complete homework assignments as well as modeling interpersonal skills. Being a parent is synonymous with being a teacher.

Never doubt your ability as a parent to be your child's best teacher.

—Karen Russell, 3 years home-school parent

EVERYONE STARTS SOMEWHERE

All teachers start somewhere. Those who select education as a profession have the foundation of years of lectures, readings, and supervised training yet still have to go through the adventure of surviving the first year of teaching. Nothing prepares one for teaching like teaching itself. The fear and anxiety that you might experience as you set about educating your own children is felt by most novice teachers as is the anticipation and excitement.

As a home educator, your intimate understanding and love for your child can help balance and enhance your lack of formal training. You may not be trained for or inclined to teach a class of second graders,

but you can sit with your own child and share your knowledge and skills. Individual and small-group instruction is a powerful educational setting. As one Arkansas home-school mom, Louise Jones, said, *I have three children and all three have different personalities, and they are all motivated differently. A classroom teacher cannot take into consideration the varying personalities of 30 students as often as the home-schooling parent can in a tutorial setting.*

Even lack of experience in a particular subject can be turned into an advantage. Sharing your lack of knowledge with your child allows you and your child to learn together. When teacher and student set out on a joint inquiry, more than just the subject is taught. The student learns that it is acceptable to admit ignorance. The student learns *how* to learn—a critical life skill which will benefit him or her throughout life. And, inspired by your enthusiasm, the student experiences the pleasure of learning.

Possessing a teaching credential is not a prerequisite to successful home education, and a parent's level of education is a minimal predictor of his or her success as a home educator (*Home School Court Report*. The Home School Legal Defense Association, December 1990, pp. 2-7). Obviously, it is easy to understand that a parent who is only semi-literate would have a difficult time teaching a child to master reading. On the other hand, it is not necessary to be a quantum physicist to succeed at home education.

Our experience in a supervisory role with home educators has shown that parental commitment and love of learning are more important than years of schooling. We have seen parents with advanced degrees burn out after less than a year while parents with only a high school education successfully home school for years. Successful home education is the result of many complex and interrelated issues, talents, and factors. A parent's attitude toward education and level of commitment to the home-schooling process is as important as his or her amount of education.

CONTINUED EDUCATION HELPS

Parents may have an intimate understanding of their children, however, that understanding may not always be enough to insure a successful home-school experience. The value of understanding ongoing research in child development, educational philosophy, and teaching methodology cannot be overstated. The more you learn about educating your child, the more your

Our experience in a supervisory role with home educators has shown that parental commitment and love of learning are more important than years of schooling.

child will benefit from home education. The references in the bibliography are a good place to start. Taking classes for credit or noncredit at your local college or university can also be a big help. Home-school workshops and conventions are offered in most areas and these can be informative, helpful, and encouraging.

I've found the single most motivating thing I can do for my children is to love to learn myself and to model for them an excitement about life and every subject they are studying.

—Linda Wevodau, 13 years home-school parent

FAMILY AND FRIENDS CAN HELP

You do not have to teach your children *everything.* Outside resources are usually an option. It is common for a home-school family to have a relative in the extended family who is willing to join in the adventure. Grandparents, friends, and even neighbors may want to share an area of expertise or interest with your child.

SUPPORT GROUPS HELP

Many parents who educate at home find other parents doing the same and find formal support groups in which parents teach their "specialties." One dad may teach a small group of children history while a mom teaches math. Addresses and telephone numbers for national and international support groups are listed on page 185.

If you don't join an organized support group, you may find it helpful to informally meet with two or three parents, perhaps over the phone. These informal meetings can offer the encouragement and support which is vital to the home-school educator. You can also talk to teachers, friends, and relatives who have knowledge about education in general or home schooling specifically. Learn all you can from their experiences, and become the best home educator you can be.

If my wife or myself is having difficulty reaching our son, we are able to talk with our assigned home-school teacher who has always been able to offer us sound and consistent advise that has helped us. —Bill Caro, 3 years home-school parent

OUTSIDE RESOURCES HELP

There are many outside resources in the community, including private tutors, local parks and recreation classes, and libraries which often have regional computer link-ups. Some families maintain a working relationship with their child's former or future public or private school, and the child is allowed to attend select classes, events, or field trips. Some parents sign up their children in correspondence programs or independent study programs provided by a district, city, county, state, or province. As Kimberlee Graves of Cypress, California, stated in her evaluation of this book, *Be sure to tell parents that some school districts offer home schooling as an alternative, complete with teacher support and curriculum materials. It would be a shame if parents didn't explore this option simply because they were unaware of its existence.*

What if I do not have family support?

When you decide to educate your children at home, you definitely take a road less traveled. You do not have to make this journey alone, but the reality is that you may not have the complete backing of family and friends.

Strength of conviction and clarity of vision will give direction to your path and help you negotiate the lonelier stretches of the road.

The decision to educate at home is much easier if you have the support and cooperation of the extended family. Home education can be stressful for home-schooling parents. Without support and encouragement from family and friends, that stress can become significantly greater. There are many ways home-school parents deal with this difficult situation.

STAY COMMITTED

Parents who make the commitment to educate at home have spent much time weighing the pros and cons. Home education is a big step, a step not to be taken lightly. This is why it is important to know exactly why you want to home educate, what you want to achieve, and how you want your children to benefit. Strength of conviction and clarity of vision will give direction to your path and help you negotiate the lonelier stretches of the road.

Home schooling, once a common practice, is still an offensive idea to some people. Though the practice of compulsory school attendance is a comparatively recent development, it is well established within our culture. Rather than seek to change these attitudes, some parents quietly do what they believe is best for their children. These parents trust that the eventual outcome in the lives of their children will be a more commanding justification for home education than words.

INVITE INVOLVEMENT

Some home-school parents enlist family involvement to alleviate concerns regarding intellectual or social development. For example, grandparents who are worried that their home-schooled grandchildren will not learn how to read are sometimes recruited as reading tutors. Grandchildren and grandparents get to spend more time with each other, and grandparents gain the opportunity to do something to ease their concerns. In addition, these experiences can bring family members closer together which may create a more positive learning environment for the child. Parents may also experience the pleasure of watching the grandparents undergo subtle shifts in attitude because of their direct involvement in home education. This is an approach by which everyone benefits.

EDUCATE

Some parents rally family support by educating family members about home schooling. They gather and distribute materials explaining the benefits of home schooling. They present home-education books as gifts. They share articles about home-school families in magazines and newspapers. They share successes of their home-schooled children and display student projects. They clarify and discuss their home-school position at family gatherings.

The subject of home schooling becomes a learning experience for all involved with the family.

JOIN A SUPPORT GROUP

Joining or starting a support group is one way to find additional encouragement. Support groups meet to share ideas, experiences, and concerns. It is a great opportunity to listen to home-school parents share teaching strategies that have worked with their children. It is also encouraging and rewarding to hear their successes and failures in this same challenging endeavor. More information about support groups is found on page 185.

I have found that when I'm discouraged, I can talk to another home-school mom and get great encouragement and practical tips.

—Elizabeth Caro, 3 years home-school parent

What are the characteristics of a successful home-school parent?

Success stories run the gamut—from the experiences of an organized, highly-structured mother of five to the tales of a creative, spontaneous single dad with his seven-year-old son.

Each family has unique gifts, abilities, and challenges. Every family also has a different view as to what comprises success. For the purpose of this discussion, we will define success in home schooling as: *Families growing closer, children and parents excited about learning together, and appropriate educational progress being made*—or, as one home-school student stated when asked about his first year of home schooling—*I liked being home because I felt happy there, and I learned a lot.*

Even using this broad definition of success, successful home-school parents share key characteristics. These key characteristics help families get established in home schooling, accomplish their goals, and stick together in tough times. The characteristics can be divided into three main categories: intrapersonal, interpersonal, and physical/material.

Intrapersonal Characteristics

A key ingredient to keeping sane and sensible while home schooling is the ability to organize. Setting goals, planning lessons, and teaching children—all while running a household—require

As a home-schooling parent, much of your time will be spent reading and learning along with your child.

organizational abilities that most CEOs would envy. However, even when organized, life seldom goes as planned, especially when children are involved. Therefore, the ability to be flexible, to change and adjust plans as needed, coupled with a sense of humor is imperative to ensure that your organized plans remain "user-friendly."

As a home-schooling parent, much of your time will be spent reading and learning along with your child. If you have a love of reading and a strong desire and enthusiasm to keep learning and growing, this aspect of home schooling will be easier for you and will be deeply rewarding.

Lastly, it's a tremendous asset to be steadfast and resolute about your conviction to home school. There may be many times during your home-school experience that you wonder aloud, *Why on earth am I doing this? Am I crazy? Sending my children to school would be much easier.* Tenacious parents deflect self-doubt and the doubt of well-intended relatives, neighbors, and friends as they set their sights on their original goal—to love, nurture, and educate their children.

INTERPERSONAL CHARACTERISTICS

Support and open communication between family members are important to the success of home schooling. Spending extended periods of time together while assuming new responsibilities will intensify the relationships in your family. A strong degree of unity between parents is a big plus. You'll need each other for support and encouragement as well as for rest and recreation breaks.

Another key factor to consider is your *desire* to spend additional time with your children. If you currently live for vacations to end so that your children will return to school, home schooling may not be the best option for you. However, keep in mind that negative behavior in some children may be reduced when children are away from peer pressure or an inappropriate educational setting. Additionally, many home-school families with more than one child discover that their children become much closer. Sibling rivalry lessens significantly as the children receive more attention from their parents.

Tenacious parents deflect self-doubt and the doubt of well-intended relatives, neighbors, and friends as they set their sights on their original goal—to love, nurture, and educate their children.

Quality education can take place in a three-room apartment or on a thirty-acre farm.

Individuals who value privacy and solitude will have some adjustments. A solo shopping trip or afternoon home alone are great luxuries. The constant company of children can be a major adjustment for novice home-schooling parents whose children have previously attended school.

PHYSICAL / MATERIAL CONSIDERATIONS

Quality education can take place in a three-room apartment or on a thirty-acre farm. However, appropriate space and adequate materials certainly make the job easier. It's also a plus if there is outside support and direction available from an independent study program, correspondence school, or home-school cooperative. In addition, the availability of transportation to field trips, the library, social events, and outside activities is a tremendous help.

CHARACTERISTICS OF SUCCESSFUL HOME-SCHOOL PARENTS

RATING
Low   High

Intrapersonal Characteristics
1. Flexibility and patience
2. Organizational ability
3. Sense of humor
4. Personal desire to grow & learn
5. Tenacity and determination

1 2 3 4 5
1 2 3 4 5
1 2 3 4 5
1 2 3 4 5
1 2 3 4 5

TOTAL _____

Interpersonal Characteristics
1. Strong relationship with spouse
2. Desire to spend extended time with children
3. Open communication between family members
4. Support from family members
5. Sensitive to needs/abilities of children

1 2 3 4 5
1 2 3 4 5
1 2 3 4 5
1 2 3 4 5
1 2 3 4 5

TOTAL _____

Physical/Material Characteristics
1. Parent at home and available to teach
2. Finances allow for parent at home
3. Space to teach
4. Ability to purchase (or borrow) appropriate materials/texts available from a local
5. Close proximity to support and direction available from a local school, independent study program, or home school cooperative

1 2 3 4 5
1 2 3 4 5
1 2 3 4 5
1 2 3 4 5
1 2 3 4 5

TOTAL _____

Highest Scoring Category: _____
Lowest Scoring Category: _____
Area(s) of Strength: _____

Area(s) of Concern: _____

NOW IT'S YOUR TURN

We've created a chart to help you evaluate yourself in light of the key elements just discussed. Take a look at each characteristic and rank yourself from 1 (low) to 5 (high) in each area. Each category has a maximum of 25 points. The higher your score in each category, the easier that aspect of home schooling will be for you. If your scores are consistently low, but you still feel a strong desire to educate your children at home—don't give up. Use this information to help you set up an action plan. We have supervised many families for whom the decision to home school was the starting point of growth in all areas of their lives. Their strong commitment to home school provided the motivation necessary to work through stressful family situations and to build strong support systems.

CHARACTERISTICS OF SUCCESSFUL HOME-SCHOOL PARENTS

	RATING Low ← → High

Intrapersonal Characteristics

1. Flexibility and patience	1 2 3 4 5
2. Organizational ability	1 2 3 4 5
3. Sense of humor	1 2 3 4 5
4. Personal desire to grow & learn	1 2 3 4 5
5. Tenacity and determination	1 2 3 4 5

TOTAL: _____

Interpersonal Characteristics

1. Strong relationship with spouse	1 2 3 4 5
2. Desire to spend extended time with children	1 2 3 4 5
3. Open communication between family members	1 2 3 4 5
4. Support from family members	1 2 3 4 5
5. Sensitive to needs/abilities of children	1 2 3 4 5

TOTAL: _____

Physical/Material Characteristics

1. Parent at home and available to teach	1 2 3 4 5
2. Finances allow for parent at home	1 2 3 4 5
3. Space to teach	1 2 3 4 5
4. Ability to purchase (or borrow) appropriate materials/texts	1 2 3 4 5
5. Close proximity to support and direction available from a local school, independent study program, or home-school cooperative	1 2 3 4 5

TOTAL: _____

Highest Scoring Category: _____

Lowest Scoring Category: _____

Area(s) of Strength: _____

_____

_____

_____

Area(s) of Concern: _____

_____

_____

_____

Home Schooling ©1995 Creative Teaching Press, Inc.

What financial aspects must be considered?

The costs involved in home schooling can vary greatly depending on the curriculum used, tuition required for support services, and the amount of resource materials purchased. Work schedules may also be affected.

Many creative parents find ways to increase family income without jeopardizing their home schooling.

REDUCED INCOME

Because one parent needs to be available on a consistent basis to provide instruction and supervision, families are generally limited to one income. Two-income families changing to one-income families will need to examine their budget carefully so that the added financial burden and lower income do not add undue stress or hardship.

Many creative parents find ways to increase family income without jeopardizing their home schooling. Some parents establish a small family business. A home business not only augments income but provides valuable learning experiences for their children. Many seek part-time jobs to do at home such as writing, editing, medical transcribing, or sewing. Some parents arrange a co-op teaching situation with another home-school family to allow for part-time employment. Many familes simply scale down their budget.

EDUCATIONAL EXPENSES

As a home-school educator, you may experience some expenses in the areas of curriculum, support services, resources materials, and field trips.

Curriculum: Some support organizations provide these materials for you free, while others charge. New, grade-specific curriculum materials can range in price from under $100.00 to over $300.00 for all subjects. The most expensive programs are prepackaged and provide extensive curriculum guides. Many home educators "pick and choose" their curriculum rather than buying all from one publisher. See pages 174–180 for an annotated list of curriculum resources.

Support Services: Support groups and private, independent study programs often charge a nominal fee of $15.00 to $50.00 monthly to maintain records and provide classes, field trips, etc. Some parents feel they need to supplement their teaching with private tutoring. Prices for individual tutoring range from $15.00 to $50.00 per hour, depending on the curriculum area and the availability and experience of the tutors.

Resource Materials: Prices for resource materials vary. Many useful and valuable materials can be borrowed or checked out from the library to avoid cost. A list of resource materials you may need is provided on page 43.

Field Trips: Field trip costs vary. Many, such as visits to the post office or tide pools, are free. You will more than likely find yourself taking advantage of your flexible schedule and taking extended field trips on a regular basis. Many home-school families take at least one field trip per week. These hands-on experiences are powerful tools for reinforcing curriculum content.

■_____

Many useful and valuable materials can be borrowed or checked out from the library to avoid cost.

■_____

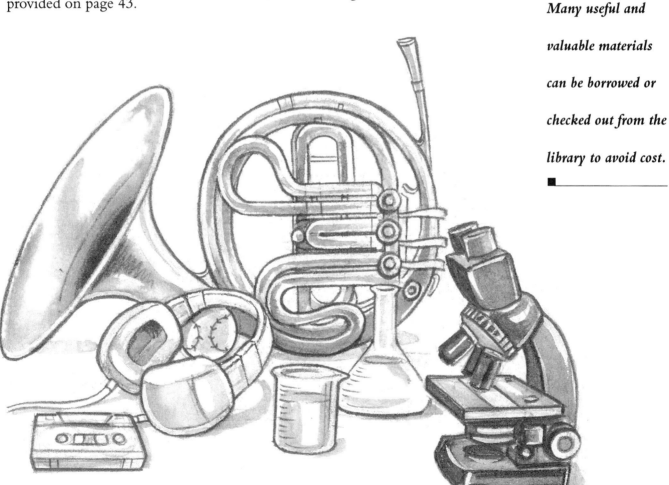

EDUCATIONAL SAVINGS

The expenses involved in home schooling are often offset when you consider the following areas:

Private School Tuition: Private school tuition generally ranges from $1,000.00 to $5,000.00 plus per year. If you are moving from private school to home school, you will experience a tremendous savings.

Day Care Expense: If you had previous day care expenses, these will most likely be eliminated or greatly reduced with one parent at home full-time.

Clothing: Home schooling can reduce clothing costs. Pressure to meet fashion trends is minimized.

Car and Mileage: If you currently drive your child to school, home schooling will eliminate this cost. However, the savings on commuting may be offset by additional driving required by field trips.

NOW IT'S YOUR TURN

Below is a cost analysis sheet for one family which compares public, private, and home-schooling expenses.

COST ANALYSIS

This cost analysis sheet is provided to help you estimate the cost of homeschooling in comparison to private and public education.

	Public	Private	Home School
Basic Academic Expenses			
Tuition	$ 0	$3,500.	$ 0
Books	$ 0	$ 185.	$ 150.
Supplies	$ 50		$ 100
Extra Curricular Activities			
Music Lessons / Rentals	$1,200	Incl in Tuition	$1,200
Sports Equipment	$ 100	$ 100	$ 100
Academic Tutoring	$1,500	$ 0	$ 200
Art Lessons	$ 200	Incl in Tuition	
Technology			
Computer Hardware	N/A Already have		$ 200
Computer Software	$ 200	$ 200	
Practical Expenses			
Lunches / Snacks	$ 650	$ 650	$ 200
Clothing / Uniforms	$ 600	$ 600	$ 300
Day Care	$1,500	$1,500	$ 300
Car and Mileage	$ 0	$1,000	$ 0
Other			$ 300
TOTAL	$6,000.	$7,735.	$2,850

A blank form is found on page 31. If expenses are an important concern in your family, it would be wise to use this tool as a financial evaluation.

A blank form is found on page 31.

> **Be sure to tell parents that some school districts offer home schooling as an alternative, complete with teacher support and curriculum materials.**
>
> —Kimberlee Graves, 2 years home-school parent

COST ANALYSIS

This cost analysis sheet is provided to help you estimate the cost of home schooling in comparison to private and public education.

	Public	Private	Home School
Basic Academic Expenses			
Tuition			
Books			
Supplies			
Extra Curricular Activities			
Music Lessons / Rentals			
Sports Equipment			
Academic Tutoring			
Art Lessons			
Technology			
Computer Hardware			
Computer Software			
Practical Expenses			
Lunches / Snacks			
Clothing / Uniforms			
Day Care			
Car and Mileage			
Other			
TOTAL			

Home Schooling ©1995 Creative Teaching Press, Inc.

The Caro Family

Bill, Elizabeth

Ryan (7)

Ashley (4)

—3 Years

Home Schooling

I enjoy having home school. It is fun. I can wake up whenever I want. I don't have to wake up at 6:30 a.m. and I don't have a new teacher every year. In home school I enjoy my sister watching us and asking questions. I like having my mom and dad for teachers. —Ryan Caro, age 7

Organization

- What does a typical day look like?

- What materials do I need?

- Where can I find curriculum materials?

What does a typical day look like?

If 100 home-school families were asked to record the schedule and activities of a typical day, the result would be 100 different sets of schedules with time spent on a multitude of subjects.

Families who choose to use traditional textbooks with correlating teacher materials often set up their morning schedule to resemble a "traditional classroom."

Describing a typical home-school day is almost as difficult as describing the characteristics of a successful home-school parent. This is due in large part to varying home-school methods. Upon close inspection three main home-schooling approaches emerge: textbook-driven, theme-driven, and interest-driven. The chosen approach largely determines the schedule and activities for the day.

TEXTBOOK-DRIVEN

Families who choose to use traditional textbooks with correlating teacher materials often set up their morning schedule to resemble a "traditional classroom." Individual subjects are taught at separate times with specific pages and objectives for each area. Seasoned home-school families quickly learn when flexibility and adaptation of materials will benefit their children. Most families find that the individual and small-group instruction possible in home school allows them to effectively cover most of the academic subjects in the morning hours. The afternoon is free for music, sports, home skills, and extra-curricular activities. Some children may choose to spend time in the afternoon to continue research or long-term projects.

The Sample Daily Schedule & Activities on page 35 describes the schedule and activities of a fifth-grade girl using a textbook-driven curriculum. She spends the morning doing text work. She discusses objectives with her mother who explains and clarifies new concepts as needed.

SAMPLE DAILY SCHEDULE & ACTIVITIES

Textbook-Driven
Fifth-Grade Student

TIME	ACTIVITIES
7:00–7:45	Dress / Household chores / Clean room / Dust family and living rooms
7:45–8:15	BREAKFAST
8:15–8:45	**Opening:** Family sharing / Religious training/values
8:45–9:30	**Reading:** Shared and silent reading
	Read Chapter Three in anthology – discuss questions
	Instructional Reading Skills: Complete reading journal, page 26
	Plot development diagram
9:30–10:15	**Writing:** Descriptive paragraph, page 20
	Spelling: Lesson Three, compound words
10:15–10:45	BREAK
10:45–11:30	**Math:** Lesson 13, pages 26–27, positive and negative numbers
11:30–12:30	**Social Studies/Science:** (rotate each week)
	Read and discuss Chapter Three of social studies text, pages 33–40
	Colonial American Heroes, Chapter 2
12:30–1:30	LUNCH
1:30–3:30	**Music:** Practice piano
	Home Skills/Art: Decorate cake for neighbor's birthday/Make birthday card
	Computer Technology: Word processing software / Educational games
3:30–5:30	FREE TIME
5:30–6:00	DINNER
6:00–8:00	**Physical Education:** Baseball

THEME-DRIVEN

Theme-driven studies use a single topic or a related series of topics as the content framework for teaching all skills and subject areas. This approach can be used to teach children at different levels simultaneously, assigning more difficult reading material and follow-up tasks to older children and easier tasks to younger children.

Most theme-driven units incorporate all academic areas. However, we recommend your family use a supplemental math program and, if necessary, a beginning reading program with your thematic units. The Sample Daily Schedule & Activities on page 37 describes how one mom coordinated the activities of her second-grade girl and fourth-grade boy. The children are currently investigating the desert habitat as part of their thematic study on *The Habitats of Our World*. Note that time blocks are larger than those in the textbook-driven schedule and often include several subjects.

Theme-driven studies use a single topic or a related series of topics as the content framework for teaching all skills and subject areas.

SAMPLE DAILY SCHEDULE & ACTIVITIES

Theme-Driven
Second and Fourth-Grade Students
Students: <u>Sarah Joy, grade 2 and Zachary, grade 4</u>   Date: <u>12-12-94</u>

7:30–8:00	Dress / Household chores / Family time
8:00–8:30	*BREAKFAST*

8:30–10:00

Language Arts
Brainstorm desert words / record on computer (2, 4)
Read *Life in the Desert* (4)
Read *Look at the Desert* (2)
Draw a picture on a postcard and write a note describing the desert to a friend who lives in Alaska (2, 4)

10:00–10:30 *BREAK*

10:30–12:00

Math
Multiplication computation drill, page 63 (4)
Addition computation drill, page 48 (2)
Graphing of desert plant and animal life (2, 4)

Science
Science experiment showing effect of wind on desert habitat (2, 4)

12:00–1:00 *LUNCH*

1:00–2:30

Social Studies/Art
Locate and identify deserts of the United States on U.S. map (2, 4)
Design desert diorama using a shoe box (2, 4)

2:30–3:00 *BREAK*

3:00–3:30

Music
Guitar lesson on Tuesday (4) / Piano lesson on Thursday (2)

3:30–5:00

Physical Education
Soccer practice (2, 4)

5:00–6:00 *FREE TIME*

6:00–6:30 *DINNER*

INTEREST-DRIVEN

There is not a typical interest-driven day. Activities and explorations can vary. The parent who takes this approach believes that truly meaningful and long-term learning occurs when the child is directing his or her own intellectual investigations. Parent-directed instruction also occurs, but usually after the child asks for direction, information, or a specific skill.

In an interest-driven schedule children spend their days reading books of their own choosing, writing stories, composing letters to pen-pals, experimenting with art, taking care of pets, running errands with their parents, visiting the library, going to the park, playing games, collecting snails, singing songs, learning to swim, visiting relatives, or going to the bookstore. One day they may be reading about Venus, the next day they may be building a three-dimensional city out of construction paper or blocks. They are free to plan a business, write a song, or play with the calculator. They can go outside and jump rope or play a math game indoors. They go about the business of life, learning and experimenting, in much the same manner as adults.

Children experiencing the interest-driven approach learn to build upon and trust their abilities and interests.

Their natural inquisitiveness is their personal and relevant course of study. In short, an interest-driven approach makes the entire world a classroom and each day an adventure.

The interest-driven approach may sound like a breath of fresh air compared to the textbook-driven and theme-driven approaches; however, the interest-driven approach is more challenging to document. A parent records learning activities in a learning log (see page 39) after the learning has occurred, rather than planning activities ahead for the child. Some planning could occur, however. For example, Tim is interested in airplanes and aerodynamics. Tim and his parents plan experiences together—trips to the remote control air flight field, buying materials ahead for flight experiments, visiting the airport, and taking a flight to visit Tim's grandparents. If the parent starts to control the planning rather than the child, you enter the realm of theme-driven.

SAMPLE LOG OF ACTIVITIES RECORDED AFTER AN INTEREST-DRIVEN DAY

NAME: Amy   **GRADE:** 3   **DATE:** 3-5-95

SUBJECT	ACTIVITIES
Reading	*Miss Rumphius* by Barbara Cooney
Handwriting	Letter to Dad / Birthday Card / Laundry basket labels
Language Skills	Granny's House: a cooperative game which teaches following directions and thinking skills
Math	Mental math: addition and subtraction with regrouping Multiplication facts 1-10 Sorting and grouping coupons / Play with calculator *Anno's Math Games* by Mitsumasa Anno
Social Studies	Family life and pioneer history *Little House on the Prairie* by Laura Ingalls Wilder
Science	*Ranger Rick*—rain forests *Tell Me Why*—scorpions *Reading Rainbow*, public television—*The Magic School Bus* (caves)
Art / P.E.	Dance Class
Other	Sewing

The log of activities for the interest-driven day was recorded *after* the learning had occurred. These were self-directed activities that the student chose based upon her interests. There are no times recorded because the learning drove the day, not the schedule. The parent recorded the learning at the end of the day and grouped the activities by subject.

interest-driven approach, a blending of approaches may be best for your children. As Susan Hayes, a home-school mom, in Milton, Washington, described, *I must be primarily a textbook-driven teacher with overtones of theme-driven and sprinkles of interest-driven.*

Both the text-driven and theme-driven programs should have an interest-driven day now and then.

A BLENDING OF THE APPROACHES

Most parents start with a textbook-driven or theme-driven approach and then work into the interest-driven approach in some or all subjects. Home schooling is a unique opportunity to tap into your child's interests. As one home-school parent said, *Both the text-driven and theme-driven programs should have an interest-driven day now and then.*

While some families enjoy a strictly

Novice home educators or families in stressed situations should not place too much emphasis on the clock. It's okay if your home schedule doesn't look like one of the three schedules just listed. Remember, the big picture is most important—*Is my child learning? Is my child making progress? Are we covering appropriate curriculum?*

On page 41 is a blank schedule for a day. Make several copies of this page and use it as a frame for planning or recording learning activities.

DAILY SCHEDULE & ACTIVITIES

TIME   **ACTIVITIES**

What materials do I need?

Gather resources for home schooling gradually. It's *not* imperative to have a fully stocked classroom on the first day.

BASIC SUPPLIES

As you get to know your child's academic needs, you'll begin to have a better idea of what materials are needed. Page 43 will help you get started. Shop at garage sales, library sales, or curriculum exchange fairs sponsored by local home-school groups. Many books and resources can be checked out from the library. Additionally, support groups and public and private independent study programs often have extensive materials available to check out or purchase.

Support groups and public and private independent study programs often have extensive materials available to check out or purchase.

METHOD-SPECIFIC MATERIALS

Your teaching approach will dictate your choice of materials. Many materials will be used with all three approaches.

Textbook-Driven: Texts and materials that match grade–level curriculum guidelines.

Theme-Driven: Books, magazines, artifacts, videos, and science supplies to correlate with each unit; grade–level math and possibly beginning reading materials.

Interest-Driven: Stimulating books, materials, and enrichment classes in the areas of your child's interest. Check your local support group and/or community services for appropriate classes.

MATERIALS CHECKLIST

BASIC SUPPLIES

- ❏ desk or table (or dining room table)
- ❏ appropriate lighting
- ❏ bookshelves
- ❏ filing cabinet (or cardboard boxes)
- ❏ cupboards/shelves (for storing educational games /manipulatives)
- ❏ answering machine (to save countless interruptions)
- ❏ cordless phone or phone with a long cord (for those times you must answer the phone)
- ❏ blackboard, white wipe-off board, or individual boards

CLASSROOM RESOURCES

- ❏ world map
- ❏ map of your country
- ❏ map of your province or state
- ❏ globe
- ❏ pencils, pens, erasers
- ❏ paper—lined and unlined
- ❏ science equipment—varies according to concepts covered

BOOKS AND REFERENCES

- ❏ grade level curriculum and resources (listed on pages 59–67)
- ❏ student dictionary
- ❏ student atlas
- ❏ student thesaurus (grade 3 and up)
- ❏ English usage handbook (grade 3 and up)
- ❏ encyclopedia set (or use the set at the library)

ORGANIZATIONAL HELPS

- ❏ large 3-ring binder for parents to keep records
- ❏ large 3-ring binder to keep each child's work
- ❏ appointment book
- ❏ large calendar (to record family activities, field trips)
- ❏ lesson plan book (forms to reproduce on pages 160–167, 172–173)
- ❏ attendance calendar (form to reproduce on page 156)

TECHNOLOGY

- ❏ computer (It's ideal to have your own—if you don't make arrangements with friends or the local library.)
- ❏ user-friendly word processing software
- ❏ developmentally appropriate computer games and curriculum support software

ART SUPPLIES

- ❏ plastic bins or shoe boxes to store art supplies
- ❏ construction paper
- ❏ scissors
- ❏ crayons
- ❏ felt pens
- ❏ watercolors/brushes
- ❏ glue sticks
- ❏ liquid glue
- ❏ tempera

Where can I find curriculum materials?

Some private schools offer home-school programs and sell curriculum materials to enrolled families. Public school home-school programs, sometimes referred to as independent study programs in the United States, distribute curriculum materials at no cost to the parents.

THE COMMUNITY

You can find curriculm materials almost anywhere. Friends and relatives may have useful books and materials. The public library is an excellent and inexpensive source for academic materials, resources, and services. Your local bookstore will carry current books and magazines addressing a variety of educational subjects. Teacher supply stores are often frequented by home-school parents. Support groups sometimes have educational swap meets where parents can buy used materials or sell books they no longer need. And, you can always look in your local telephone book under "School Supplies."

TEXTBOOK PUBLISHERS

The curriculum resources listed on pages 174–180 are publishers and distributors of textbooks, supplemental educational materials, aids, and resources. Some of the materials are specifically designed for home-school families. Most of the companies listed publish catalogues. Call or write to find out if the catalogues are free or if there is a small charge. You would also be advised to contact textbook publishers in advance to find out their policies for private schools and home schools. Some textbook publishers will sell materials only to schools or teachers employed by schools.

Support groups sometimes have educational swap meets where parents can buy used materials or sell books they no longer need.

Experienced home-school parents tend to buy from several curriculum sources, based upon the individual needs and interests of their children.

SCHOOL DISTRICT

Some school districts rent or loan textbooks, and some districts sell old texts and teachers' manuals for very low prices (which can be supplemented by up-to-date library resources). Experienced home-school parents tend to buy from several curriculum sources, based upon the individual needs and interests of their children. A caution for novice home educators—don't invest too heavily into a whole system of curriculum materials from one publisher. Pick and choose based upon *your* child's needs.

INDEPENDENT STUDY AND CORRESPONDENCE PROGRAMS

If you prefer to have someone else choose your curriculum materials for the first year of your family's home-schooling experience, you may want to formally enroll in an independent study program or correspondence school. It is imperative to contact your local authorities to see what types of programs meet state or provincial guidelines. For example, in California, enrolling in a correspondence school would *not* meet compulsory attendance laws, whereas in British Columbia, enrolling in correspondence school *would* meet regulations. A word of caution—laws are always changing. Write or call your local agency for updated information.

The Lee Family

John, Juanita

Jonathan (9)

Evan (7)

Brett (4)

4 Years

Home Schooling

We chose to home school under an umbrella program, rather than independently, so that our children could be home schooled with some of the benefits that an organized program could offer. These benefits include choral groups, musical and drama performances, public speaking, computer classes, foreign language classes, field trips, science fairs, and intramural sports. Other benefits of an umbrella program include: in-servicing for parents, home visits by credentialed teachers, standardized and diagnostic testing, and assistance with legal questions. —John Lee, home-school dad

Legal Requirements

- What are the legal requirements for home schooling?

- What records do I need to keep?

What are the legal requirements for home schooling?

While legal requirements vary, most governments require notification and many require verification that your child is making appropriate progress in the home-school setting.

CERTIFICATION

Write your local, state, or provincial government agency to find out any legal requirements *you* must meet in order to qualify as a home-school educator. You will find a listing of agencies by state and province on pages 181–184. Most regions allow a child to be educated at home by tutors as well as parents. Your state or province may or may not require the tutor or parent to be a certified teacher. Some areas require only that parents are "competent." Other areas want parents to have a high school diploma or bachelor's degree, pass the GED (Graduation Equivalency Diploma), or take a proficiency or competency exam. At present in Canada, no province specifies through legislation, regulation, or policies any requirements with respect to the qualifications of home-schooling parents or guardians.

It is essential that you contact local authorities to confirm that what you are doing is legal.

NOTIFICATION/APPROVAL

In the United States, notify your local public school principal, local school board, county superintendent, or state department of education of your intention to home school with an affidavit or a letter of intent. In Canada, contact the Ministry of Education or Department of Education to find out requirements. Some provinces have "approval laws." Approval is obtained from a superintendent, director of schools, or directly from the department of education. Some provinces allow registration with independent schools as an additional option. Some states or provinces require a specific form to be filled out; whereas others simply require a letter stating your intent to home school. It is essential that you contact local authorities to confirm that what you are doing is legal.

In the United States, your state may consider your home school to be a private school or allow you to acquire such designation. In many cases, states may not regulate private schools. You might be able to home educate by enrolling in a correspondence school, a private school satellite, or an independent study program. There are a growing number of public school, independent study programs designed to help home-education families.

Currently in Canada, Ontario is the only province that has home-educating parents register as a private school. In Canada, some provinces, such as Saskatchewan, allow parents to use the provincial correspondence materials to home educate their children. These correspondence materials are basically the same materials as those used in public schools. Other provinces, such as British Columbia, do not consider use of correspondence materials to constitute home educating but rather to be public schooling through distance education.

TESTING

In the United States, some states stipulate periodic standardized testing. Sometimes the parents can choose the test. The administrator of the tests may be a parent, a certified teacher, district personnel, or a "neutral" person. Some states or provinces keep the test scores on file. Other states act upon the test scores: children who score below a certain level can be returned to school, placed on a one-year probation, or tested further for learning disabilities. Testing information can be found on pages 186.

In Canada, most provinces and territories have no testing requirements for home schooling. In Alberta, as of fall 1994, home-schooled children must be assessed by the parents; parental assessments must be submitted to the supervising board or private school. The students must also be tested at their grade level and at the time designated by the minister for grades 3, 6, and 9. The students take the Alberta achievement tests and other provincially mandated tests unless the minister exempts the student. In Newfoundland, testing may be requested as part of the supervising board's assessment of a home-school student's progress. A few provinces such as British Columbia, Saskatchewan and Yukon Territory allow parents to request access to testing at their discretion. In most cases, it will be provided.

RECORDS

In the United States, some states, such as California, request files to be kept that include proof of immunization, work samples, and evaluation of progress such as test results or written summary evaluations. These files are kept in a cumulative record. Parents, certified teachers, or licensed psychologists can be assigned to keep the files.

In Canada, Alberta and Saskatchewan require that records are kept. These records are called the portfolio of student work. Some provinces, such as Alberta, Prince Edward Island, Saskatchewan, and Nova Scotia, require one or two reports annually to document home-schooled students' progress. British Columbia requires no testing, no submission of student work, no annual reporting, and no monitoring or home visitations by school district staff.

It is essential that you write your state or province for current and exact requirements. Laws and regulations are constantly changing. Required record keeping will be discussed in more detail in the following section.

Laws and regulations are constantly changing.

What records do I need to keep?

Record keeping is a time-consuming task but may be important for verifying your child's educational experience.

Write or a call your state, province, or home-education association to get the most updated information for your area.

Record-keeping requirements for home schooling vary. Write or call your state, province, or home-education association to get the most updated information for your area. In Canada, ask for the Education or School Act and the applicable regulations or statutes dealing with home education or home-based learning. Most Canadian provinces and territories have *no* requirements for record keeping. Some states require that the following records be kept: cumulative records, a course of study, immunization and health records, attendance records, and evaluation records. Many home-school families in Canada and the United States keep records, required or not, for their own purposes of documentation.

CUMULATIVE RECORD OR PORTFOLIO OF WORK

In the United States, a cumulative record is initiated when a child enters a public or private school. The cum file, as it is often called, usually contains a summary of grades, attendance, and test scores as well as comments and observations on the child's academic and social progress. The cumulative record follows the child from K-12 and is transferred by mail to each school the child attends. In Canada, the child's main academic record is more commonly called a portfolio of student work.

If a cumulative record or portfolio of work is required in your area, maintain your child's file or initiate the file when your child begins kindergarten. If you join a public or private independent study program or a home-school cooperative, cumulative records are often maintained for you as part of the services provided. If you are home schooling independently, blank cumulative record files can be purchased through:

Bob Jones University Press
Greenville, SC 29614
(800) 845-5731

If your child has already been in a public or private school, you will need to send the school a letter requesting that cum records be sent to you. Write the letter on your school stationery or type the name and address of your school at the top of the page. If you return your child to a public or private day school, simply register your child at the school office. Do not bring your child's cums with you at this time. Wait for the formal request and then send the cum by mail.

In Canada, the term "portfolio of student work" replaces the term "cumulative record." The three maritime provinces—New Brunswick, Newfoundland, and Prince Edward Island—as well as the Northwest Territories do not address home schooling in law or regulations to the extent that the other provinces and territories do; however, some are currently undergoing a process of amending legislation and/or statutes.

If you join a public or private independent study program or a home-school cooperative, cumulative records are often maintained for you as part of the services provided.

COURSE OF STUDY OR EDUCATIONAL PLAN

The majority of states require that a course of study be completed for each home-schooled student. In Canada, the course of study would be most commonly called the educational plan. The course of study often includes all subject matter you plan to cover as well as the texts and/or materials you plan to use. The sample course of study to the right was planned for a fifth-grade student who is primarily using a textbook-driven curriculum with a literature-based reading program.

Turn to page 157 for a blank Course of Study form. Keep in mind that this form is not standardized but will help you organize and record your curriculum content.

The course of study often includes all subject matter you plan to cover as well as the texts and/or materials you plan to use.

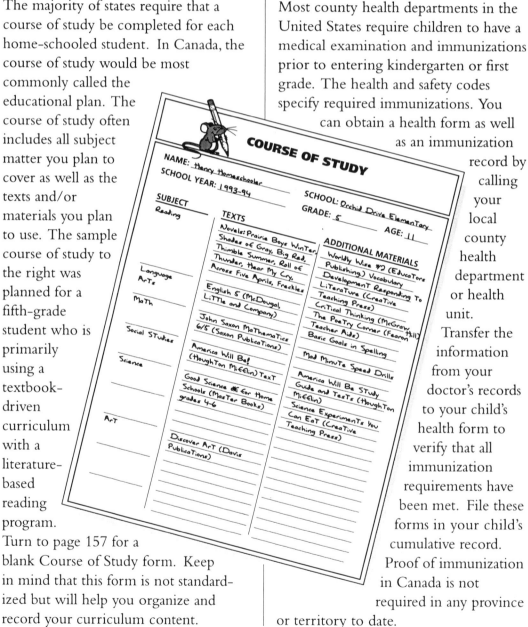

COURSE OF STUDY

NAME: Henry Homeschooler
SCHOOL YEAR: 1993-94
SCHOOL: Orchid Drive Elementary
GRADE: 5
AGE: 11

SUBJECT — TEXTS

Reading
Novels: Prairie Boys Winter,
Shades of Gray, Big Red,
Thimble Summer, Roll of
Thunder, Hear My Cry,
Across Five Aprils, Freckles

Language Arts
English 5 (McDougal,
Little and Company)

Math
John Saxon Mathematics
6/5 (Saxon Publications)

Social Studies
America Will Be!
(Houghton Mifflin) Text

Science
Good Science & for Home
Schools (Master Books)
grades 4-6

Art
Discover Art (Davis
Publications)

ADDITIONAL MATERIALS
Worldly Wise #2 (Educators
Publishing) Vocabulary
Development, Responding To
Literature (Creative
Teaching Press)
Critical Thinking (McGraw Hill)
The Poetry Corner (Fearon
Teacher Aids)
Basic Goals in Spelling

Mad Minute Speed Drills

America Will Be Study
Guide and Tests (Houghton
Mifflin)
Science Experiments You
Can Eat (Creative
Teaching Press)

IMMUNIZATION AND HEALTH RECORD

Most county health departments in the United States require children to have a medical examination and immunizations prior to entering kindergarten or first grade. The health and safety codes specify required immunizations. You can obtain a health form as well as an immunization record by calling your local county health department or health unit.

Transfer the information from your doctor's records to your child's health form to verify that all immunization requirements have been met. File these forms in your child's cumulative record.

Proof of immunization in Canada is not required in any province or territory to date.

ATTENDANCE CALENDAR

Most states require an attendance calendar be kept as a record of days of academic instruction. In Canada, however, home educators are not required to record or submit the total number of days of academic instruction, although one province, Quebec, does specify 180 days. Check with your state or province to find out current requirements and to see if a specific form must be used for attendance records. Academic years range from 175 to 195 days in North America.

should be typed or neatly printed in black ink. Write an E for "entered" on the first day of instruction. After the "E" record a slash mark for each school day attended. Indicate holidays with an "H" and sick days with an "S." The attendance calendar should also be kept in your child's cumulative record. Refer to page 156 for a blank form.

Most states require an attendance calendar to be kept as a record of days of academic instruction.

Many independent study programs provide attendance calendars based on the public school's academic year. Use a calendar like the one shown below for a traditional school year (September through June) or for year-round instruction. The top portion of the attendance calendar

EVALUATION

It is helpful to include some form of evaluation in your child's permanent record, although not all states or provinces require it. If you desire a formal record, report cards can be developed or purchased. A written summary of a child's progress, especially for primary grades, may offer the most practical value.

Anecdotal records (day-by-day notes) and portfolios are used widely as a form of evaluation. For example, Mrs. Miller keeps a weekly sample of her son's writing along with her written observations in a portfolio to document his writing progress. Greg's science experiments and models are photographed and his social studies plays (written by Greg and performed with siblings and friends) are videotaped. These photos and tapes are kept in Greg's science and social studies portfolios. For further information on using portfolios, read *Portfolio Assessment* (Creative Teaching Press, 1992).

Detailed portfolios for each subject can be cumbersome. It is helpful to decide how often to insert something in your child's portfolio. For example, you might choose to insert one sample from your child's best work in each subject each week or each month. This helps control the paper volume. At the end of the year, you and your child may choose to leave in only two or three work samples.

forms like them to keep records of your children's schooling. Laws can change radically from year to year. If you are ever asked to document your child's learning, you will have thorough records of your child's progress.

We advise using these forms or forms like them to keep records of your children's schooling.

This evaluation is a simple year-end summary but can also be used on a semester, quarterly, or term basis. Minimally, we suggest you keep the information called for on this form for your child's cumulative record. Refer to page 158 for a blank evaluation form. Evaluation will be discussed in more detail on pages 112–115.

Even if your state or province doesn't require all of the forms mentioned, we advise using these forms or

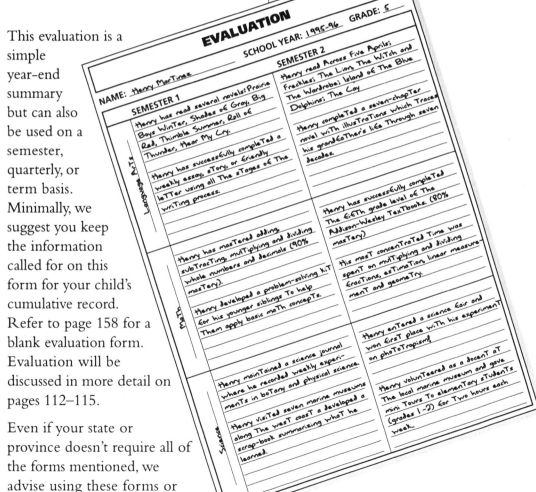

The White Family

Steve, Sharon

Kirsten (15)

Justin (13)

Brendan (9)

—*10 Years*

Home Schooling

If I could give one piece of advice to a new home-schooling mom it would be to be flexible! I have learned that if I meet a lot of resistance with an assignment, my children are usually not being obstinate; they just don't have the skills to finish the task or I haven't explained it properly. If I set the assignment aside for a period of time or if I change the assignment to teach the same skill in a different way, I have more success. —Sharon R. White, home-school mom

Curriculum and Instruction

- What curriculum should I teach?

- What does my child need me to teach?

- How does my child learn?

- What instructional approach should I take?

- How do I match my instructional approach to the required curriculum?

- How do I plan a textbook-driven program?

- How do I plan a theme-driven program?

- How do I plan an interest-driven program?

- How do I teach several children at once?

- How do I motivate my child to do the work?

What curriculum should I teach?

State and provincial curricular guidelines vary; however, there are certain concepts and skills generally suggested or required for grades K–8.

Maturation, different educational approaches, and repetition all work together to help "turn on the lights" for our children.

—Christy Cech, 5 years home-school parent

It should be noted that some states and provinces do not legally require a specific course of study or educational plan to be followed in the home-school setting. These states and provinces take a more "hands-off" approach. The grade-level lists on the following pages are not meant to be a rigid set of rules but are meant to serve as a general guideline. Christy Cech, a home-school parent with five years of experience, puts curriculum requirements in perspective: *As a new, insecure home-schooling parent, I often worried that my children would not completely master educational concepts being introduced at their grade level. I pictured a house being built that had to have every brick in place at the foundation level. If I missed a brick in kindergarten, I was convinced that the house would topple! I didn't realize there was so much repetition in education, especially in the early years. I finally understood that if my child didn't "get it" one year, they might "get it" the next or the next! Maturation, different educational approaches, and repetition all work together to help "turn on the lights" for our children.*

The following pages contain general curricular guidelines for K–8 only. Standards vary greatly at the high school level and students may choose specializations which affect their curricular requirements. A more comprehensive course of study guide can be purchased for a nominal price from World Book Educational Products.

United States Address:
World Book Educational Products
101 North West Point Blvd.
Elk Grove Village, IL 60007

Canadian Address:
World Book Educational Products
257 Finchdene Square, Unit 2
Scarborough, Ontario
MIX IB9

Some states, such as Arkansas, offer a guide as to what content should be offered at each grade level. Some home-school companies offer scope-and-sequence charts. The following pages provide a broad overview of the basic concepts generally taught in language arts, math, social studies, and science.

Kindergarten

 **LANGUAGE ARTS**

Reading readiness activities

Beginning phonics

Listening to literature

Following and giving directions

Paraphrasing and summarizing

Language-experience stories

 MATH

Counting 0-20

1-to-1 correspondence

Equal to, greater than, less than

Simple addition

Simple subtraction

Calendar use

Time to the hour

Problem-solving with addition, subtraction

Introduction of money denominations

Basic shapes

Estimation

Number line

⊕ SOCIAL STUDIES

Holidays, traditions, cultures

Community

Self-study/self-esteem

Rules that protect us

Locations/simple maps of home / neighborhood

Familiarization with other cultures

Basic land forms

 SCIENCE

Classification skills

Seasonal changes/weather

Five senses

Farm animals

Pets

Simple measurement

Light

Introduction to the scientific processes

First Grade

 **LANGUAGE ARTS**

Basic word-attack skills

Basic sight-word vocabulary

Introduction to writing process

Writing simple sentences and stories

Introduction to literary concepts
(authorship, title, illustrations, story
order)

Manuscript writing (printing)

Beginning spelling

Speaking and listening skills

$$\frac{1}{2} < \frac{3}{4}$$
$$\frac{1}{4} + \frac{1}{3}$$ **MATH**

Counting and writing to 100

Place value

Addition and subtraction through 18

Basic fractions

Use of number line

Monetary denominations

Problem-solving

Ten as a base unit

SOCIAL STUDIES

Basic history of country

Holidays, traditions, and customs

Community helpers

Characteristics of town and country

Characteristics of city and suburb

Basic geography/mapping skills

 SCIENCE

Simple machines

Animals

Air and water

Magnets

Scientific processes

Solids, liquids, gases

Solar system

Second Grade

LANGUAGE ARTS

Mastery of basic word-attack skills

Extended sight-word vocabulary

Silent reading for specific purposes

The writing process

Writing paragraphs, letters, journals, and simple book reports

Literary concepts/terms (plot, setting)

Dictionary skills

Introduction to basic grammar

Basic punctuation

$\begin{array}{|c|} \hline 2 \times 2 \\ 3 \times 3 \\ \hline \end{array}$ MATH

Place value

Mastery of addition facts to 18

Mastery of subtraction facts to 18

Multi-digit addition and subtraction

Basic fractions

Problem solving

Number line

Simple charts/graphs

Measurement

Introduction to multiplication

Use of calculator

SOCIAL STUDIES

Parents, grandparents, ancestors

Communities in other lands

Community helpers

Citizenship/responsibility

Maps/globes

⚛ SCIENCE

Water cycle

Life cycles

Plants and animals

Dinosaurs

Habitats and homes

Climate

Gravity

Useful/harmful animals

Scientific processes

Third Grade

 **LANGUAGE ARTS**

Silent reading

Oral presentations

The writing process

Writing paragraphs, short stories, letters, journals, poetry

Literary concepts/terms (simile, idioms, metaphor, personification, imagery)

Punctuation

Basic grammar

Spelling

Cursive writing

Dictionary skills

Listening/speaking skills

 **MATH**

Place value

Addition and subtraction with renaming

Basic multiplication facts

Basic division facts

Introduction of long division

Basic geometry

Graphs/charts

Fraction comparisons

Problem-solving

Estimation

Use of calculator

 **SOCIAL STUDIES**

Local history/geography

Famous historical figures

Traditions

Patriotic celebrations

Basic North American geography

Flat maps/globes

 **SCIENCE**

Habitats

Energy

Conservation

Magnets and electricity

Light and color

Force and work

Scientific method and processes

Fourth Grade

 LANGUAGE ARTS

Silent reading

Critical reading skills (main idea, cause/effect, drawing conclusions)

Oral reading/presentation

Introduction to literature genres

Literary concepts/terms (conflict, theme, characterization, alliteration, rhyme, rhythm)

Listening/speaking skills

The writing process

Writing personal narratives, directions, tall tales, simple reports, book reports, poetry

Dictionary/research skills

Basic grammar

Vocabulary/word study skills

Spelling

Punctuation

 **MATH**

Place value

Four basic operations $(+, -, \times, \div)$

Decimals/fractions

Estimation

Ratios

Averages

Graphs/charts

Basic geometry

Prime factoring

Use of calculator

 SOCIAL STUDIES

State or provincial history and geography

Time zones

Longitude, latitude, scale

 SCIENCE

Solar system

Classification systems

Environment of local state or province

Earth's atmosphere

Earth's resources

Human body

Ecosystems

Basic biology

Scientific method and processes

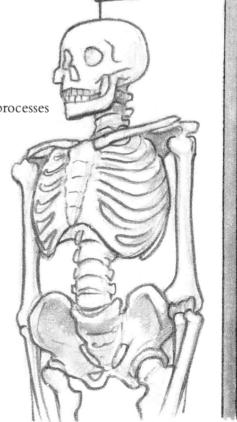

Fifth Grade

 **LANGUAGE ARTS**

Silent reading

Critical reading skills expanded (bias, inferences, judgments)

Oral reading/presentations

Literary concepts/terms (point of view, tone, mood, style)

Literature genres

Study skills

Spelling

Paragraphs (topic sentence, supporting sentences)

Dictionary skills

Basic grammar

Punctuation

The writing process

Writing narratives, instructions, book or movie reviews, fables, descriptive writing, short stories, research reports, poetry

 **MATH**

Four basic operations ($+$, $-$, x, $\div$)

Place value

Decimals

Multi-step word problems

Measurement

Ratio

Percents

Fractions

Symmetry and congruence

Area and volume

Factoring

Exponents

Use of calculator

Probability

 SOCIAL STUDIES

North America past and present

North American geography

Principles of democracy

 **SCIENCE**

Animal and plant classification

Human body systems

Land forms/changing earth

Space/space exploration

Weather and prediction

Scientific method and processes

Sixth Grade

 LANGUAGE ARTS

Silent reading

Oral presentations/creative dramatics

Critical reading skills

Literary concepts/terms
(foreshadowing, flashbacks, symbolism)

Spelling

Mastery of basic grammar (eight parts
of speech)

Types of literature

Study skills

Research skills

The writing process

Writing descriptions, persuasive essays,
business letters, short stories, character
sketches, expositions, poetry

$\boxed{c = \pi \times r^2}$ MATH

Basic operations ($+$, $-$, x, $\div$)

Multiplication (up to three-digit
multiples)

Division (up to three-digit quotients)

Place value

Factors

Decimals

Fractions ($+$, $-$, x, $\div$) with mixed
numbers

Ratio

Percents

Geometry

Area/volume

Use of calculator

Integers

Exponents

Probability

SOCIAL STUDIES

World history, ancient civilizations from
early Middle Eastern civilizations to the
rise of the Roman Empire

World geography

Political and economic systems

Mapping skills

Ω SCIENCE

Classification of plants/animals

Electricity

Magnetism

World climates

Energy

Simple astronomy

Properties of light

Scientific method and processes

Seventh Grade

 **LANGUAGE ARTS**

Silent reading (novels, plays, poetry, ballads, legends, mythology)

Critical reading skills (relationships, varied reading rates)

Literary terms/concepts reviewed

Extended research skills (atlases, encyclopedias, directories)

Advanced grammar (clauses, gerunds, phrases)

The writing process

Writing news articles, narratives, persuasive essays, short stories, poetry

Oral presentations and creative dramatics

 MATH

Extended review of four basic operations (+, -, x, ÷)

Decimals

Fractions

Measurement

Ratio/proportions

Percent

Geometry

Volume

Statistics and graphs

Probability

Integers

Equations with integers

 **SOCIAL STUDIES**

World history from the fall of Rome to the civilizations of the Americas

Environment

World geography

SCIENCE

Earth science introduction

Scientific classification

Atmosphere/air pressure

The cell

Laws of motion

Scientific method and processes

Heredity and genetics

Eighth Grade

LANGUAGE ARTS

Silent reading (novels, biographies, narrative poetry, nonfiction narratives)

Oral presentations/creative dramatics

Critical reading skills (inductive and deductive reasoning)

Advanced grammar (infinitive, participle, gerund, predicate nominative, predicate adjective)

Literary terms/concepts reviewed

Extended research skills

The writing process

Writing reports, plays, short stories, poetry, feature stories, business letter, descriptive writing, narratives

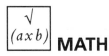 MATH

Review of basic operations of whole numbers (+, -, x, ÷)

Review of decimals, rounding, estimating

Expressions/equations

Integers

Number theory

Fractions (+, -, x, ÷)

Exponents

Ratios, proportion

Percent

Geometry

Square root

Statistics

Probability

Algebra

SOCIAL STUDIES

Canadian or United States history

Advanced North American geography

Canadian or United States political system

Canadian or United States Constitution/government

SCIENCE

Astronomy

Space

Conservation

Motion

Machines

Periodic table of elements

Compounds and mixtures

Chemical changes

Scientific method and processes

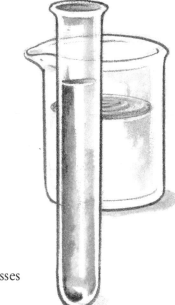

What does my child need me to teach?

Analyze your child's strengths and weaknesses before purchasing curriculum materials to help you develop a tailor-made program.

Page 69 shows a record of the strengths and weaknesses of a fourth grader named Jessica. Jessica is a good oral reader but does not particularly enjoy reading. Her parents provide high-interest reading materials slightly below her reading level, so Jessica can read faster with more enjoyment and with improved accuracy. Her confidence leads her to select reading materials at a more advanced level.

Since Jessica loves writing poetry but has difficulty completing a project, her parents help her publish a poetry journal. They break assignments down into small, manageable blocks. Jessica's mother helps her edit her work. The individualized guidance and incremental approach helps Jessica learn how to break down a large, demanding task.

Since Jessica has excellent computational skills but is weak in application, her parents provide opportunities in real-life problem solving. They begin a family business called *Crazy Cookies.*

Jessica learns how to multiply recipes, keep a ledger, and calculate costs and profits.

To capitalize on her interest in geography, Jessica makes a bulletin board featuring a world map. Each week Jessica finds a newspaper article that highlights a different country. A colored piece of yarn links the country with the article. Jessica's world awareness increases and her reading fluency improves as well.

Remain flexible and adapt your curriculum to your child, not the other way around

—Karen Russell, 3 years home-school parent

68

Jessica's parents help her maintain a strong social network while also encouraging her to work independently on special interest projects. They suggest she take tennis and swim lessons at the community recreation center. In addition, they hope to spark an interest in science by enrolling her in a summer science series offered by a local arboretum. By taking time to analyze their daughter's strengths and weaknesses, Jessica's parents are successfully developing a program tailor-made for Jessica.

NOW IT'S YOUR TURN

Complete My Child's Strengths and Weaknesses assessment sheet found on page 159 for each child you will be teaching. Record general thoughts rather than details. The completed form can serve as a broad reference tool to assist you in selecting materials that target your child's needs.

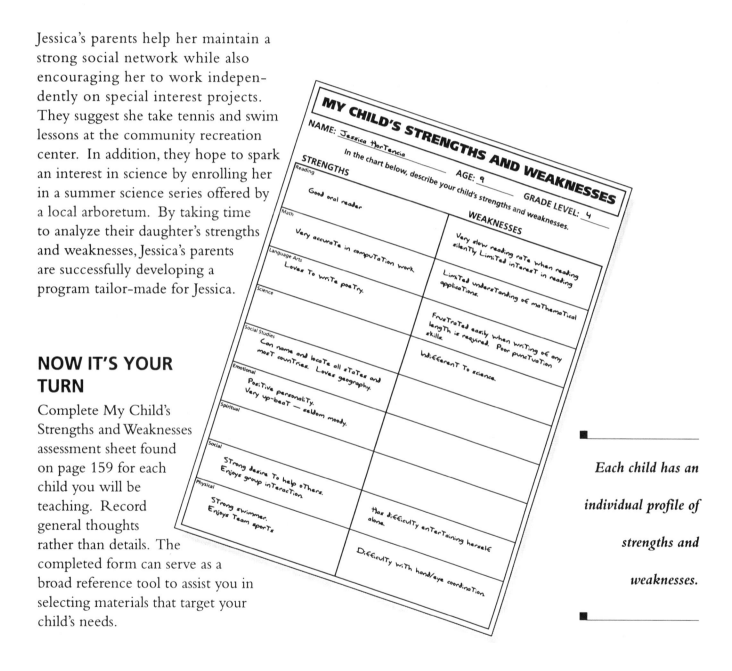

MY CHILD'S STRENGTHS AND WEAKNESSES

NAME: Jessica HorTencia

In the chart below, describe your child's strengths and weaknesses.

AGE: 9   GRADE LEVEL: 4

STRENGTHS	WEAKNESSES
Reading Good oral reader	Very slow reading raTe when reading silenTly. LimiTed inTeresT in reading.
Math Very accuraTe in compuTaTion work.	LimiTed undersTanding of maThemaTical applicaTions.
Language Arts Loves To wriTe poeTry.	FrusTraTed easily when wriTing of any lengTh is required. Poor puncTuaTion skills.
Science	IndifferenT To science.
Social Studies Can name and locaTe all sTaTes and mosT counTries. Loves geography.	
Emotional PosiTive personaliTy. Very up-beaT — seldom moody.	
Spiritual	
Social STrong desire To help oThers. Enjoys group inTeracTion.	Has difficulTy enTerTaining herself alone.
Physical STrong swimmer. Enjoys Team sporTs.	DifficulTy wiTh hand/eye coordinaTion.

Each child has an

individual profile of

strengths and

weaknesses.

How does my child learn?

Understanding your child's learning modality, temperament style, and areas of intelligence will help you structure your child's education in a way that makes learning easier, more rewarding, and more meaningful.

As a home educator, you have the opportunity to acknowledge each child's unique learning style and to incorporate that style into the instructional format.

Every child has his or her own unique way of learning. Parents with more than one child observe this fact on a daily basis. One child may love to complete workbook pages and memorize spelling words while that child's sibling may find this type of work aggravating. As a home educator, you have the opportunity to acknowledge each child's unique learning style and to incorporate that style into the instructional format.

There are several useful theoretical frameworks that can be used when considering your child's particular learning styles.

LEARNING MODALITIES

Modalities are the sensory channels (visual, auditory, and kinesthetic) we use to acquire and process information.

- *Visual learners* learn best by observing demonstrations or by seeing pictures and diagrams.

- *Auditory learners* learn best by listening and discussing.

- *Kinesthetic learners* learn best by doing.

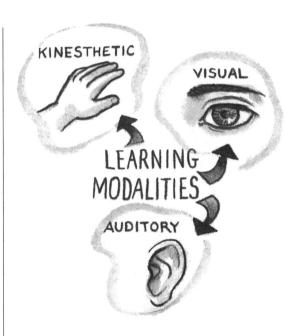

If your child's strongest learning modality is kinesthetic, he or she may learn the alphabet best by tracing letters in sand; whereas a visual learner may recall what an *A* looks like simply by seeing it in a book. An auditory learner may recall every detail of a book read aloud; whereas a visual learner may require seeing the print and pictures to retain the information. Some elements of all three learning modalities are evident in most learners. As you choose curriculum, keep your child's learning style in mind.

TEMPERAMENT STYLES

Temperament theory acknowledges that we differ in our interests, perceptions, judgments, and attitudes. Temperament style also affects the *way* we learn, *what* we want to learn, and *how* we want to learn (Kiersey, David and Marilyn Bates. *Please Understand Me.* Prometheus Nemesis Books, 1984). There are four basic components to temperament style:

WHERE ATTENTION IS FOCUSED

- *Extroversion:* Focuses attention on the outer world of people, events, and objects.

- *Introversion:* Focuses attention on the inner world of ideas.

HOW INFORMATION IS ACQUIRED

- *Sensing:* Acquires information directly through the senses. Focuses on the concrete and the present.

- *Intuition:* Acquires information through insight, inspiration, and hunches. Focuses on the possible and the future.

HOW DECISIONS ARE MADE

- *Thinking:* Makes decisions based on logical analysis and consideration of cause and effect.

- *Feeling:* Makes decisions based on personal values and a consideration of how the decisions will affect self and others.

WORK HABITS AND LIFESTYLE

- *Judging:* Prefers life to be orderly and planned.

- *Perceiving:* Prefers life to be spontaneous and flexible.

Understanding the differences in temperament styles helps you understand the approach your child brings to learning which may be completely different from your own or that of other children in your family. Understanding your child's temperament style helps you most effectively plan his or her learning activities.

*Temperament style affects the **way** we learn, **what** we want to learn, and **how** we want to learn.*

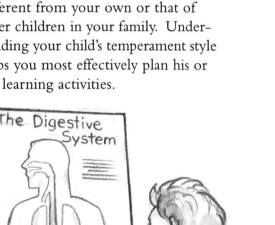

INTELLIGENCE

Howard Gardner, the originator of the theory of multiple intelligences, has described a model of thinking that encompasses at least seven different kinds of intelligence. These areas of intelligence are defined as follows:

1. **Verbal-Linguistic:** Speaking and reading.

2. **Logical-Mathematical:** Forming concepts and finding abstract patterns.

3. **Visual-Spatial:** Thinking in images, pictures, shapes, and colors.

4. **Musical:** Rhythm, pitch, melody, and harmony.

5. **Bodily-Kinesthetic:** Touching, manipulating, moving, making, and doing.

6. **Interpersonal:** Relating to and cooperating with people.

7. **Intrapersonal:** Independence and self-motivation.

Your child will most likely choose a career that calls upon his or her greatest talents.

Your child may be particularly intelligent in one or two areas while struggling in another. Understanding these strengths and weaknesses gives you insight into how your child learns and where he or she may need the most educational support. For example, if your child is strong in logical-mathematical but weak in verbal-linguistic, you may need to spend additional time in language arts. However, keep in mind that while you want to strengthen deficits, you also want to reinforce strengths. Your child will most likely choose a career that calls upon his or her greatest talents. For further reading on multiple intelligences, read Gardner's *Multiple Intelligences: The Theory in Practice*.

These frameworks are not all-inclusive and do not imply an either-or situation. We all possess to some degree all the various components. The idea of learning styles acknowledges that for each of us some of these components are more highly developed than others. As a result, we generally have a preferred learning modality, temperament style, or intelligence type. The visual learner, for example, can process auditory information, but his or her *preferred* modality is still visual. The *preferred* modality is more efficient for the learner. When we are aware of our children's strongest learning modalities, temperament style preferences, and intellectual strengths and act upon this knowledge, learning can be maximized. For further reading on this topic, consider the writings of Thomas Armstrong, David Keirsey, or Dawna Markova. *The Way They Learn* by Cynthia Tobias is a particularly user-friendly source. See annotations in the bibliography.

When we are aware of our children's strongest learning modalities, temperament style preferences, and intellectual strengths and act upon this knowledge, learning is maximized.

What instructional approach should I take?

The approach you take will ideally be the one that makes learning easier and more engaging for your child.

We gave you a brief description of the three basic instructional approaches (textbook-driven, concept-driven, interest-driven) as well as a blending of these approaches on pages 34–40 when we described the typical home-schooling day. Practically speaking, the approach you choose will be the one that makes learning easier for your child as well as the one with which you are most comfortable, at least at the start. Remember that home education is a process that demands constant evaluation. Just because you start your home-education experience with a particular approach does not mean that you cannot change your mind. As the old home-schooling adage goes—*if it's not working, try something else.*

In the next several pages, we will consider some of the pros and cons of textbook-driven, concept-driven, and interest-driven approaches.

THE TEXTBOOK-DRIVEN APPROACH

A textbook-driven approach bears a remarkably close resemblance to the traditional classroom. Materials, activities, and schedules are very similar. The curriculum is presented as individual subjects. Parents use traditional school or school-like textbooks and related workbooks as the primary teaching materials.

ADVANTAGES OF THE TEXTBOOK-DRIVEN APPROACH

• This approach looks and feels like a traditional classroom. For parents who are planning to home school for a short time, this approach may make the transition to a traditional classroom easier.

• Because textbooks cover the curriculum requirements at a specific grade level, parents using this approach can be assured that they are covering most of the concepts and skills to which their children would be exposed in school.

• It is somewhat easier to plan. Most of your content information is in the textbook. Many teacher's manuals give suggested schedules and provide remedial and enrichment activities. However, keep in mind that you can vary or supplement the structure you are given.

DISADVANTAGES OF THE TEXTBOOK-DRIVEN APPROACH

- Textbook-driven instruction can present subjects in isolation with little attempt to address unifying ideas or themes. This makes understanding more difficult.

- It can be very expensive to purchase a complete grade-level curriculum and related workbooks; however, some umbrella programs will provide the textbooks for you.

- Textbook-driven instruction can be more complicated and time-consuming if you have several children at different grade levels.

- This approach may not take full advantage of home-education possibilities: flexibility, variety, and individualization.

- It is easy to place too much emphasis on drills, worksheets, and the read-the-chapter-and-answer-the-questions approach to teaching.

- This approach tends to emphasize rote memory learning instead of understanding.

THE TEXTBOOK-DRIVEN APPROACH CAN WORK WELL WITH CHILDREN WHO:

- Enjoy workbooks.

- Have a long attention span.

- Recall details and facts accurately.

- Enjoy repetition and routine.

- Work in a steady, sequential manner.

- Are task-oriented.

- Want to please.

- Prefer expectations for work to be clearly defined.

- Like to work toward a specific goal and reach it.

- Need and enjoy structure and predictability.

- Like to complete assignments on time.

- Tend to be orderly, organized, and systematic.

- Enjoy reading and writing.

- Are obedient and conforming.

- Enjoy the traditional school setting.

The textbook-driven approach can work well with children who need and enjoy structure and predictability.

THEME-DRIVEN INSTRUCTIONAL APPROACH

A theme-driven approach builds the curriculum around a number of preselected themes or topics. Parents select these themes with the input of their children. Generally, parents use a combination of traditional and non-traditional materials and activities. Children are to be involved from the selection of the topic through all succeeding phases, including gathering materials and information, designing and completing projects, and selecting methods of presentation. Methods of presentation might include audio cassette, video, dramatization, written prose, poetry, booklets, newspapers, letters, graphs, charts, photographs, slides, scale models, crafts, or any combination of these.

A theme-driven approach builds the curriculum around a number of preselected themes or topics.

ADVANTAGES OF THE THEME-DRIVEN APPROACH

- This approach integrates subjects. An integrated curriculum under a unifying theme(s) can result in more meaningful and effective instruction.

- Your child's interests can be a foundation for the curriculum.

- It is easier to teach several children at different grade levels.

- This approach lends itself to inventive activities and long-term projects.

- Planning can be an enjoyable experience that reflects the individual interests and hobbies of you and your child.

DISADVANTAGES OF THE THEME-DRIVEN APPROACH

- Planning can take more time and requires a creative and imaginative touch. Some thematic curriculum materials have done most of the planning for you.

- You must gather a variety of materials and resources. This can be expensive and time-consuming.

- It is not always possible, or at least easy, to tie in all subject requirements to the main themes. Textbooks or other supplemental materials might be needed.

- You might spend a great deal of time planning what you believe to be a fascinating and important unit, only to find that the unit is not interesting to your child.

THE THEME-DRIVEN APPROACH CAN WORK WELL WITH CHILDREN WHO:

- Want to know how subjects and ideas relate to each other.

- Need to know how topics, subjects, and skills affect themselves and others.

- Enjoy subjects and topics that concern people.

- Like to have a say in the educational decision-making process.

- Learn best when they see the "big ideas."

- Enjoy studying a topic in depth.

- Have a long attention span for specific topics.

Many families plan special culminating events for their theme-driven units. Jenni Key, a parent with nine years of home-schooling experience shares some specifics: *The end of any unit study on a country is a great excuse for a culinary adventure. We'll check the library for recipe ideas and music from a country, then surprise Dad with a meal to remember. We've listened to German polka music and eaten sausages, sauerkraut, and* apfelkuchen; *we've listened to Chinese folk music while stir frying in the wok; we've enjoyed a full English tea and readings from Christopher Robin; and we've traveled to a local Indian restaurant to sample from their buffet. Parents and kids enjoy this type of unit closure.*

The end of any unit study on a country is a great excuse for a culinary adventure.

—Jenni Key, 9 years home-schooling parent

Readiness varies

from child to child.

Parents who take

this approach believe

that there is no

preordained body of

facts that need to be

taught at set grade

levels.

INTEREST-DRIVEN INSTRUCTIONAL APPROACH

An interest-driven or child-centered approach gives your son or daughter the opportunity to select what is learned and when it is learned. Parents postpone formal instruction until they decide that their child is ready. Readiness varies from child to child. Parents who take this approach believe that there is no preordained body of facts that need to be taught at set grade levels. The primary goal is for the child to experience the pleasure of learning for as long as possible. In this way, the child acquires a lifelong inclination to learn.

ADVANTAGES OF THE INTEREST-DRIVEN APPROACH

- This approach requires little or no academic planning.

- Your child learns to become an independent learner.

- This approach minimizes conflict between you and your child over instructional issues.

- Your child's learning experiences are natural and immediate.

- This approach maximizes student interest which results in more learning.

- Your child has the opportunity to become an expert in whatever he or she chooses.

- Your child's entire environment becomes the classroom; all experiences are learning experiences.

DISADVANTAGES OF THE INTEREST-DRIVEN APPROACH

- This approach requires parents to have a broad knowledge of curriculum content. Parents must be able to record at the end of the day their child's learning activities and the relationship the activities have to required curriculum.

- This is the most misunderstood instructional approach. It can be difficult to manage and difficult to explain to others.

- Your child may appear to be "behind" others of the same age in some subject areas, because your child is not following the same scope and sequence.

- This approach requires trust in your child's ability to teach himself or herself. It also requires patience while your child follows his or her own time sequence.

- You must put up with your child's fluctuating interests and bursts of energy. They are normal. For example, some children will read voraciously and exclusively but never pick up a pencil to write. Then, as if determined by some inner developmental clock, they will set aside their books and write for weeks at a time (stories, lists, letters, plans, poems, songs).

- You will feel like you are homesteading the library.

THE INTEREST-DRIVEN APPROACH CAN WORK WELL WITH CHILDREN WHO:

- Dislike routine.
- Ask a lot of "why" questions.
- Enjoy learning new skills more than practicing old ones.
- Enjoy delving into a topic (formally or informally).
- Work in bursts of energy.
- Find paper and pencil work deadly.
- Receive information from hunches and intuitive leaps.
- Need variety.
- Are imaginative and creative.
- Like to follow inspirations and instincts.
- Like opportunities for being inventive.
- Do not work sequentially.
- Are curious and spontaneous.
- Have a strong sense of self-direction.

- Like to move around and explore.
- Are self-motivated on projects of their own choosing.
- Do not respond well to too much structure.

Remember, that the best instructional approach for your family may not be textbook-driven, theme-driven, or interest-driven. The best approach for your family may be a combination of approaches. You may vary the approach depending upon the subject or the child. The beauty of home schooling is its flexibility. Do what is best for your family and at the same time meet any requirements of your state or province.

Learning never stops: child-directed learning eases into adult-directed learning so that individuals view learning as a continuous lifelong process.

—Debby LaRoy, Canadian Home Educators' Association President

79

How do I match my instructional approach to the required curriculum?

You can meet your child's specific educational needs by using a textbook-driven, theme-driven, or interest-driven approach—or a combination of the three.

The following description explains how the three main approaches can be used to match grade-level requirements.

TEXTBOOK-DRIVEN

If you are using a textbook-driven approach, most of your curriculum planning has been done for you. Textbook publishers incorporate appropriate content and activities to meet the major requirements generally required for each grade level. If you use a grade-level textbook from a major publisher, you will most likely meet the requirements for that subject at that grade level. This is one of the appealing features of a textbook-driven approach.

Overreliance on textbook publishers to determine the appropriate content of your child's study can be a risky feature of this approach. It is easy, especially for beginning home-education parents, to allow the required skills to become their primary focus. Parents sometimes elevate the content of the textbooks

over the needs of their child. It is easy to slip into the routine of reading a chapter a week or completing a set number of workbook pages a day. Work samples are generated; tests are administered and scored; textbooks are completed. If you take a textbook-driven approach, it is important to periodically review your home-education goals. Ask yourself: *Is my child benefiting from this routine? Is my child progressing academically? Is my child enjoying the home-education experience? Am I?* Textbooks are a tool to reach a goal, not an end in themselves.

Textbooks are a tool to reach a goal, not an end in themselves.

THEME-DRIVEN

A successful theme-driven, home-education experience requires a great deal of advance planning. You will need to select the themes you will be exploring; gather the materials and supplies you will need; and plan related activities, projects, and assignments. You also must figure out how these plans can meet your state or province's grade-level requirements. If you review requirements ahead of time, you can incorporate them in assignments, projects, and activities.

For example, let's say you plan to develop a teaching unit around the topic of spiders for a third-grade child.

Below is a partial listing of typical third-grade language arts requirements with matching theme-driven activities.

Most parents who use a theme-driven approach successfully find a match between the required curriculum and their theme activities. Some requirements (i.e., multiplying three-digit numbers) may not fit into a unit theme. When this occurs, use supplemental materials or activities so that your child covers all concepts required at his or her grade level. Math, particularly for older students, often requires specific lessons.

A successful theme-driven, home-education experience requires a great deal of advance planning.

REQUIREMENTS	MATCHING ACTIVITIES
Write a personal story.	✔ Write about a real-life experience involving spiders.
Write a book report.	✔ Write a report on a book about spiders.
Write a personal letter.	✔ Write a letter to a relative or friend describing what you have learned about spiders.
Write a descriptive paragraph	✔ Write a paragraph detailing how a spider spins a web.
Write a creative story.	✔ Write a story about a boy or girl who becomes a spider for a day.
Write a research report.	✔ Write a report about poisonous spiders summarizing what you have learned from books, videos, and field trips.

INTEREST-DRIVEN

By definition, the interest-driven approach places emphasis on the child's curiosity. This child-centered approach places a great importance on the process of learning. As with all approaches, intellectual independence and a lifelong love of learning are the desired outcome.

As mentioned on page 38, parents taking an interest-driven approach find it easier to use activity logs instead of lesson plans. Activity logs are a record of how the child spends his or her days. The activities, once logged, can then be defined in terms of grade-level require-ments. Below is an example of a day's logged activities for a first-grade child and the educational requirements that those activities meet.

During an average day, children's activities are many, varied, and complex. The activities listed below met requirements in language arts, math, science, social studies, art, and physical education. When parents view their children as self-learners, they can see that many, if not all, of their children's activities are educational. Their children's daily adventures may not look like traditional schooling, but meaningful and long-term learning takes place.

When parents view their children as self-learners, they can see that many, if not all, of their children's activities are educational.

ACTIVITIES	REQUIREMENTS MET
Drew a picture of the family cat	✔ Art: drawing a picture
Dictated a letter to Mom for his grandparents and then copied the letter in his own printing	✔ Language Arts: writing a friendly letter, printing, oral language skills
Asked Mom to read a story about dinosaurs	✔ Language Arts: story appreciation, listening skills, reading ✔ Science: animals
Played with his blocks	✔ Math: counting, sorting, making designs or patterns, use of manipulatives
Went to the store with Mom, used a calculator to figure price total	✔ Math: comparison shopping, unit pricing, addition, calculator use
Went to the park and played tag with siblings and friends.	✔ Social Studies: community living, occupations
	✔ Physical Education: cardiovascular fitness

AN ECLECTIC APPROACH

Please keep in mind that your instructional approach may be a blend of textbook-driven, theme-driven, and interest-driven. For example, Sally, age seven, is in her sixth month of first-grade home schooling. She is learning her reading, writing, listening, speaking, art, and science content through a thematic marine biology unit. Her math studies and her private music lessons are textbook-driven. She receives her physical education through a community ballet program which she attends three times per week. Her social studies content is learned through an interest-driven approach. She asks a lot of questions around the holidays and she is constantly asking to go on a "trip." Mom and Dad and Grandma and Grandpa take turns accompanying her on field trips. They have taken her to two local museums where she explored and learned hands-on lessons about the indigenous people of her area. Sally has also visited community helper organizations this year—the fire department, police department, and post office. Mom, Dad, Grandma, and Grandpa all keep anecdotal notes recording discussions and experiences. Each month Mom goes through the learning log, reads the notes, and records curriculum requirements met.

How do I plan a textbook-driven program?

Advanced planning helps minimize the "tyranny of the urgent" and helps maintain your focus on the BIG picture—a balanced study that will be most meaningful and helpful for your child.

Experiences such as measuring, reading cookbooks, studying road maps, or discussing city boundaries reinforce and expand textbook lessons.

—David and Lisa Stough, 7 years home-school parents

Ideally, the first steps in planning an effective program should take place days or even weeks before your child first opens a book. The time you spend planning ahead will save countless hours later. Initial planning can feel like an overwhelming task. It's often at this point that a parent's early enthusiasm wanes.

If you have chosen to use a traditional textbook curriculum and you find yourself lamenting, *Help! What do I do with this stack of books?*, the following steps might assist your planning.

TWO TO THREE MONTHS BEFORE INSTRUCTION

Purchase or order curriculum materials. If you are ordering by mail, allow two to six weeks for delivery. Order texts for each subject area. Support personnel from independent study programs can offer a great deal of assistance in this area and, in many instances, actually provide the textbooks for you. In some cases there is no charge.

FOUR WEEKS BEFORE INSTRUCTION

Overview the curriculum. Familiarize yourself with the curriculum. Don't begin your actual plans at this point. Rather, skim through the student texts and accompanying teacher's manuals. Your goal should be to get an overview of the concepts and skills that you should cover. As you review the materials, consider them in light of your child's interests and abilities. Ask yourself the following questions:

- Will these concepts be easy or difficult for my child?

- Have any of these concepts already been introduced or mastered?

- How much follow-up practice is provided for each lesson?

- Will the amount of practice be too much or too little for my child?

- What basic teaching strategies are suggested?

- How will my child respond to these strategies?

You might not be completely sure of the answers to these questions at this point. That's okay! They are provided to help you review the curriculum in light of *your child's needs* and to assist you in using these resources to meet those needs. Hopefully, you had a chance to begin this process before you purchased the material so that you could choose materials that support your own basic approaches and philosophy.

Divide the material into manageable time blocks. Dividing material into manageable monthly or quarterly time blocks will help your BIG picture take form and structure. Long-term planning sheets with monthly blocks are provided on pages 160–161 to assist you. The sample below is for a third-grade student using a traditional textbook approach. Keep early plans *fluid* and *flexible*.

Some complete curriculum packages already have this lesson planning completed. However, we suggest you review and revise these plans to accommodate *your* child's needs and *your* schedule.

Divide each text into semester, quarter, or weeks to ensure that you'll cover all the material over the course of the year.

—Louise Jones, 2 years home-school parent

LONG-TERM PLANNING

List concepts/topics you will cover each month. You may wish to specify chapter units or page numbers.

AUGUST

Reading:
Language Arts:
Math: NO SCHOOL
Social Studies:
Science:

SEPTEMBER

Reading: Text: chapters 1-2
Language Arts: Novel: *Ralph S. Mouse*
Math: Text: unit one (sentences basic punctuation)
Composition: personal narrative
Social Studies: Chapters 1-2, pages 2-36
Science: Text: chapter 1 - George Washington
Text: chapters 1-2
habitats, desert, wet lands

OCTOBER

Reading: Text: Chapter 3
Language Arts: Novel: *A Grain of Wheat*
Math: Text: unit two (commas, verbs)
Composition: writing directions, "how to"
Social Studies: Chapter 3, pages 38-56
Science: Text: chapter 2, Paul Revere
maps and globes, pages 4-27
Chapters 3-4
habitats, rain forests, redwoods

NOVEMBER

Reading: Text: Unity
Language Arts: Novel: *The Secret River*
Math: Unit 3 adjectives, fact/opinion, contractions
Social Studies: Unit review, pages 57-60
Science: chapter 4, pages 62-83
Text: chapter 3 - Betsy Ross
maps and globes, pages 28-44
Chapter 5
habitats, wet lands

DECEMBER

Reading: Text: none
Language Arts: Novel: *The Very Best Christmas Pageant Ever*
Math: Text: none
Composition: My Best Christmas Family Traditions
Social Studies: Chapter 5, pages 84-96
Science: Christmas around the world
Tide pools

JANUARY

Reading: Text: unit 5
Language Arts: Novel: *Crow Boy*
Math: Unit 4 - pronouns, prefixes, suffixes
Composition: business & friendly letters, thank-you cards
Social Studies: Chapter 6, pages 97-102
semester review - pages 103-104
Science: Chapter 4 - Benjamin Franklin
maps and globes, pages 45-61
Chapter 6
conservation

Arrange topics of study into convenient and meaningful time periods for your teaching schedule. For example, if you are planning a week-long trip to the seashore, teach the unit on oceanography prior to or during your visit. Many topics in science do not need to be taught in the order they are presented in the textbook. Don't feel you need to address all the areas in the same depth

provide a basic structure, but remember, the joy of home schooling is the opportunity to tailor the schedule to *your* child's needs. Your child's individual needs, not the textbook publisher's schedule, should be your primary concern. So don't be surprised if you need to adjust your planning sheets at the end of the first month or two. Seasoned teachers constantly adjust

covered in the science text. Rather, you might choose to go into greater depth in an area of particular interest to your child, supplementing the text with library books and resource materials.

A word of caution is in order as you are scheduling lesson plans. Just because the textbook indicates your child should learn long division in two weeks doesn't mean he or she will. In fact, we can almost guarantee he or she won't. Monthly time blocks for planning

plans to meet the needs of their students. The longer you teach your child, the easier the planning process will be.

Decide on an appropriate daily/weekly schedule. Once you have made your BIG picture plan, it's time to define the specifics. Now is the time to think through what you will be doing each day and when you will do it. Here are some questions to ask yourself:

- What time of day will I begin instruction?

- What subjects will be taught daily?

- When will chores and other responsibilities be accomplished?

The number of children in your family and your other responsibilities will influence your schedule. Some families enjoy scheduling textbook work for Monday through Thursday to make Friday available for hands-on experiences, unit studies, or field trips. Start with the plan you think will work best for your family; if the plan doesn't fit, adjust it later.

Begin gathering resource materials and supplies. Teachers need a variety of materials at their fingertips. The list on page 43 will help you get started. If you begin to gather basic materials ahead of time, you will have time to borrow from friends and comparison shop. You will have time to see what might be available for checkout from local support organizations such as public or private independent study programs.

TWO WEEKS BEFORE INSTRUCTION BEGINS

Develop weekly lesson plans for each child. You can copy the form provided on page 165 or purchase a daily lesson plan book at a local teacher supply store. The sample lesson plan on page 89 reflects plans for a third-grade student. Your plans require only enough information to indicate your direction.

Most textbooks provide guidelines for how much to cover in each lesson (i.e., two pages of math daily). Use the textbook suggestion as a guide—unless it's already obvious to you that this will never work with your child—and make adjustments as needed. It may take weeks or even months to accurately predict your child's learning rate, so we recommend making detailed plans for a week or two at a time.

Basic subjects such as reading, writing, and math should be covered daily. Healthy living habits, such as exercise and proper nutrition, are concepts that should be practiced and learned daily through helping your child make good choices. Some subjects, such as social studies or science, may only need to be scheduled two or three times a week.

DURING AND AFTER INSTRUCTION

As your child completes a lesson, check it or highlight it on the lesson plan. If a lesson or activity is not completed, return to it the next day or eliminate it if your priorities change. The most experienced teachers consistently adjust and fine-tune their plans to allow for learning rates, review, and those wonderful, irreplaceable, teachable moments.

Evaluate your plans daily in light of your child's needs and *trust your instincts.* Remember, you are *not* required to follow a typical classroom routine. If your child has mastered a skill, why waste his or her time completing 20 more pages of tedious review? Or, if he or she can grasp a new math concept using a game or real-life situation, why assign 30 more workbook problems?

Textbooks are only one tool for learning. Used wisely, they provide a meaningful framework for a creative, individualized learning environment. If misused, they can sap your child's curiosity and rob him or her of an exciting learning adventure. Always keep in mind your original goals for home schooling your child. Let your child's needs dictate your lesson plans, not the textbook.

WEEKLY ASSIGNMENT SHEET

NAME: Michael Hage   GRADE: Third   WEEK OF: Sept. 13-17

SUBJECT	MONDAY	TUESDAY	WEDNESDAY	THURSDAY	FRIDAY
Reading	(In Good Company) Nate The Great Goes Undercover pgs 1-12	Discuss Theme, characTers NaTe The GreaT pgs. 13-25	Vocabulary word bank NaTe The GreaT pgs. 26-36	Discuss ploT developmenT NaTe The GreaT pgs. 37-49	WriTing: WhaT made NaTe The GreaT, greaT?
Language Arts	InTroduce pg 6 componenTs of personal narraTive Topic senTence	Rough DrafT Personal narrative →	Proofread and ediT	Final DrafT Personal NarraTive	Oral PresenTaTion of NarraTive
Math	lesson 1 pgs. 2-3 numeraTion →	pgs. 4-5 →	pgs. 6-7 Addition review →	pgs. 8-9 →	Marcy Cook Tiles GianT Dice
Social Studies	ChapTer one: WashingTon Carver pages 3-18 →		Begin Time line of Carver's life →	→	ChapTer summary quesTions, pg 18 (Discuss orally)
Science	ChapTer 1 DeserT HabiTaT pages 8-26 →			→	Make deserT diorama
Art, Music, P.E., Health, Other	Piano lessons Hockey PracTice	Library	Hockey PracTice	4-H club	Hockey Game

89

How do I plan a theme-driven program?

Preparation for a theme-driven study is exciting, stimulating, and often time-consuming. With advance planning, you can gather appropriate resources to personalize a unit to meet your child's needs.

Integrating social studies, science, reading, and literature into one study has been fascinating for our children.

—David and Lisa Stough, 7 years home-school parents

The following steps will help you organize and plan thematic units.

TWO TO THREE MONTHS BEFORE INSTRUCTION BEGINS

Decide if you will purchase thematic materials or design your own units. If you decide to purchase theme units, there are currently a wide variety of choices available for published theme-driven units. See pages 174-180 for listings and addresses. These materials vary in cost, topics, background research, and lesson plan guidance. Tapes and pamphlets outlining specific topics and teaching methods are usually available from the publisher for a nominal cost. Thoroughly examine these descriptions prior to making your selection. Purchase a unit that highlights topics of interest and importance to you and your child and activities that meet your teaching style and your child's learning needs. If ordering by mail, allow two to six weeks for delivery.

If you decide to design your own theme studies, you will first need to decide on the topics to be covered. Just about any area of interest to you or your child can be turned into an effective unit study. One family took two years to study the United States' presidents and their wives. They researched significant historical events to re-enact and record on time lines. The children read, discussed, and summarized numerous books and prepared favorite recipes of the presidents to serve at parties where guests wore period costumes.

Another family took a year to study the habitats of the world. Each child compiled a scrapbook with a section for each habitat. Each section contained maps, terrain and climate statistics; listings of plants and animals found in each habitat; related newspaper articles; and a journal record of the results of correlating science experiments.

As you're considering themes to study, be sure to include your child in the planning. Your child's ideas may need to be refined and organized but his or her interest will ignite the learning process and help keep your whole family challenged and motivated.

Once you have determined the theme(s) you will teach, decide what additional texts and materials are needed to round out your program. Explore libraries, teacher supply stores, and educational supply catalogues. Also, consult with colleagues. Talk with other home-school parents as well as teachers in your support group, umbrella group, or independent study program who have taught a similar unit. They may have resources you can borrow or suggestions for sources.

FOUR WEEKS BEFORE INSTRUCTION BEGINS

Complete a Yearly Planning Sheet. Write the unit(s) in the approximate time periods in which they will be covered. The sample depicts a sample half-year plan for a third-grade student. In this sample, additional materials were added to the plan to provide sequential math instruction. Blank forms for your use are provided on pages 162-163. For your own child, make an estimate of the time you will need for each section of your theme. For example, if you are studying marine

biology, consider: *Should I spend one week or two months on tide pools?* The age of your children and the materials available to you, as well as your interests and expertise, will be significant factors in determining the length of each theme study.

You are not obligated to rigidly follow this planning sheet, so don't feel guilty if your theme study doesn't correlate perfectly with the calendar months and/or your original plans. Remember, *you* are developing these plans so *of course* you can change or adjust them as needed. The purpose of the planning sheet is to assist you in recording your vision for the year and in developing reasonable yearly goals.

In a theme-driven study, our children, David and Chelsea, see how subjects are interrelated. This helps them retain information easier than in a textbook-driven approach.

—David and Lisa Stough, 7 years home-school parents

YEARLY PLANNING SHEET
Theme-Driven

Unit Concept:
AUGUST
Math Concepts:
Other: NO SCHOOL

Unit Concept:
SEPTEMBER
Math Concepts: Habitats: Oceans
Other: Chapters 1-2
Numbers addition/subtraction facts
Hands-on science at arboretum

Unit Concept:
OCTOBER
Math Concepts: Habitats: Rain Forest
Other: Chapter 3, pages 38-56
Geometry and review
Hands-on science at arboretum

Unit Concept:
NOVEMBER
Math Concepts: Habitats: Woodlands
Other: Unit review, pages 57-60
Chapter 4, pages 62-83
Begin gymnastic lessons

Unit Concept:
DECEMBER
Math Concepts: Holiday Celebrations
Other: Chapter 5, pages 84-96
Addition with renaming
Christmas boutique and street fair
(Prepare for colonial booth)

Unit Concept:
JANUARY
Math Concepts: Habitats: The Desert
Other: Chapter 6 — semester review
pages 97-104
Gymnastic lessons

Develop a planning sheet for the first section of your theme. For example, if your long-term unit theme is weather, the first section of your unit might be the sun and the seasons. Brainstorm ideas for books, activities, experiments, and writing experiences that relate to your initial unit and record them on the unit planning sheet. Teacher supply stores and catalogues have inexpensive theme books with programs already planned for you. These theme books, in addition to activities, often provide annotated lists of fiction and nonfiction books that correlate with historical and scientific themes.

Theme-driven studies use a single topic or a related series of topics as the content framework for teaching all skills and subject areas.

If this process seems difficult at first, we guarantee that ideas will be generated by even the youngest family member once you get started. This sample Unit Planning Sheet represents a unit plan for a third-grade student. A blank form is provided on page 164.

If you have purchased theme materials, you may not need to devise your own planning sheet. Publishers often do this for you.

Decide on appropriate daily/weekly schedule. Now that the overall plan is sketched, you are ready to think through what you will be doing each day and when you will do it. Ask yourself: *What time of day will I begin instruction? How will I integrate the various subjects throughout the theme? When will children attend to chores and other responsibilities?*

UNIT PLANNING SHEET

DATES: March 1995

UNIT: WeaTher

Reading Materials

Independent:
WeaTher Proverbs
STorm Warning Tornadoes and hurricanes

Read Alouds
Cloudy wiTh a Chance of MeaTballs

Social Studies:
WeaTher around The world
NorThern and SouThern Hemispheres
The Sun and The Seasons

Art: WeaTher Diorama

Music: Compose simple lyrics and melodies of weaTher songs

Cooking: Cloud cookies
LighTning Lemon Bars

Physical Education: Game: Thunder and LighTning Race

Related Field Trips: Ride in hoT air balloon

Language Arts / Writing Activities:
WriTe song lyrics for weaTher songs
Haiku
WriTe suspense sTory involving a flood.

Science: WeaTher forecasTing

Math: WeaTher measuremenTs:
baromeTers
ThermomeTers
hydromeTers
anemomeTers

Graph daily weaTher paTterns

Supplies Needed:
baromeTer (balloon, jar, sTraw)
ThermomeTer
hydromeTer
anemomeTers (wood, paper, nails)

OTher:
WeaTher sTaTion

The number of children in your family as well as your other responsibilities will affect how you arrange your schedule. Some families enjoy scheduling paper/pencil work for Monday through Thursday, with Friday available for hands-on experiences and field trips. Others enjoy hands-on experiences on a daily basis. Start with the plan you think will work the best for your family, and keep in mind that you may adjust it later.

Collect related materials. Borrow or purchase related resources for your theme units. Look for items such as maps, artifacts, books, and magazines. Mix genres of literature to give your child a broad base of nonfiction and fiction. Nonfiction books for your family to study together, related fiction to read aloud, and books for your child to read independently enhance a theme. Seriously consider literature with hands-on activities related to science, art, math, music, and cooking.

Mix genres of literature to give your child a broad base of nonfiction and fiction.

ONE TO TWO WEEKS PRIOR TO INSTRUCTION

Organize lesson plans. After you've determined your units of study and have brainstormed countless related activities, your family room may look like a cross between a used bookstore and an eclectic thrift shop. Now is the time to make use of all those wonderful ideas and your collection of assorted treasures. Armed with your first Unit Planning Sheet or the sugges-tions provided in your purchased materials, divide activities into a weekly plan. You may want to use the Weekly Assignment Sheet provided on page 165 or you may wish to purchase a lesson plan book purchased from a local teacher supply store. The sample weekly lesson plan above records the weekly plans of a third grader.

Don't feel that you need to record something in every subject every day. Some days students will benefit from a longer study of one subject area. Initially you should allow more time than you think you will need for each activity—everything in life usually takes longer than we think it will!

WEEKLY ASSIGNMENT SHEET

NAME: Amy Samuelson GRADE: Third WEEK OF: Sept. 13-17

SUBJECT	MONDAY	TUESDAY	WEDNESDAY	THURSDAY	FRIDAY
Reading	Read Independently "Big Al" Read Aloud:Where The Waves Break"		Vocabulary word bank:Add new words from story	Discuss and summarize "Big Al"	Make Triorama depicting highlights of story.
Language Arts	Begin Research on Sea Animal Visit Library	Rough Draft Report	Finish Rough Draft. Proofread and edit	Final Draft	Oral Presentation
Math	Textbook Work pgs 2-3 numeration	pgs 4-5	Text pgs 6-7	Measurement. use yard To measure size of whales	
Social Studies	Locate major ocean on globe	LocaTe major oceans and gulfs		Make world map labeling oceans and gulfs	
Science		Study ocean life food chain		Make mural illustrating ocean food chain	Cabrillo Museum field Trip
Art, Music, P.E., Health, Other		Sand arT painting		WaTer safety class at YMCA	

DURING AND AFTER INSTRUCTION

Keep track of work completed. As your child completes an activity or project, highlight it or check it off on the lesson plans. If something is not completed on a given day, evaluate its significance and either delete it or add it to the next day's work.

Relax and regroup. If your lesson plans look like a piece of fiction by the end of the week, relax . . . and regroup. Teaching a theme-driven curriculum is hard work and it takes lots of time. Your child is not just learning isolated topics. Rather, he or she is learning to reason, think, and apply information that is relevant and meaningful. You are beginning a learning adventure with your child. The *process* of this adventure is the key to producing an honest to goodness lifetime learner!

Constantly evaluate the effectiveness of your program. Students do not learn in a linear fashion. They take leaps and jumps and move all over the place in their learning. Sometimes, in the midst of a long unit, we find that our children suddenly have a grasp of the content and skills and the unit is no longer appropriate. The student may be ready to move on to a more in-depth topic. If this happens, move on. Always keep in mind that the child's needs should drive the program, rather than the program drive the learning experience. It is better to conclude a unit while your child's interest is still high than to continue a unit too long.

It is better to conclude a unit while your child's interest is still high than to continue a unit too long.

How do I plan an interest-driven program?

A parent cannot plan an interest-driven program—it happens spontaneously. Children pursue their interests and seek information through first-hand observations, experiences, and research.

An interest-driven approach postpones formal instruction until the parents see that their child is ready.

Melinda sees a caterpillar in the backyard. Melinda shows an interest in the caterpillar and a spontaneous lesson occurs on the life cycle of a butterfly. Daily observations are recorded by Melinda in her science journal and the next day she checks out several books to read about butterflies. Mom or Dad takes on the role of guide and scribe. They record Melinda's learning after the fact and identify specific curricular requirements met in her learning log. The interest-driven approach requires parents to transcend commonly accepted beliefs about the role of teacher. It also requires a strong belief and trust that children can, and do, teach themselves. In addition, the interest-driven approach requires a parent who is knowledgeable or interested in a wide range of topics.

Those parents who choose an interest-driven approach are not necessarily against lesson plans or academic skills. It's primarily a question of timing. An interest-driven approach postpones formal instruction until the parents see that their child is ready. They believe a child is ready for instruction when he or she asks for it. When a curious child asks how to pronounce or spell a word, he or she is ready for direct instruction. This is the time to teach. The information is important to the child now; it is needed now; it is wanted now. The direct instruction occurs quickly. The focus is on the enjoyment of the story or the completion of a letter, not on the acquisition of an isolated word attack skill or phonic rule.

If you are considering taking an interest-driven approach, the following steps can be helpful. Many of these steps will also be helpful for the textbook- and theme-driven approaches.

TWO TO THREE MONTHS (OR YEARS) BEFORE "INSTRUCTION"

Read a lot. Read about child development. Read about brain research. Read about home-school families. Read about interest-driven learning. *Growing Without Schooling* and *Home Education*

Magazine are helpful publications. Read about the Colfax's experience in home education. Read one or two of Raymond and Dorothy Moore's books. Read about Nancy Wallace's experiences. See the bibliography for specific titles. You can never start reading too soon; and when you are done reading, read some more.

Watch your child. Observe his or her daily activities. Begin to see these activities in terms of learning experiences. What is he or she doing? What is he or she learning?

Get in the habit of answering your child's questions directly and briefly. If your child asks how to say or spell a word, give the answer. Don't ask him or her to sound

it out or to try it. This interferes with the comprehension and enjoyment of reading or writing. It is a small accomplishment if a child learns the mechanics of reading and writing but loses the inclination to do so.

Set goals. What goals do you have for your children? Parents taking an interest-driven approach generally state they want children who:

- Are independent learners.

- Are curious.

- Are confident.

- Are not afraid to make mistakes.

- Love to learn.

- Are competent in reading, writing, and math.

- Understand citizenship and work to contribute positively to society.

Write down your goals. Refer to your goals frequently to keep focused on why you chose to use the interest-driven approach and why you chose to home school.

> *Kids need time for a relaxed, unpressured childhood.*
>
> —Susan Hayes,
>
> 4 years home-school
>
> parent

TWO TO FOUR WEEKS BEFORE "INSTRUCTION"

Get a library card and locate several bookstores. Buy a large canvas bag or get a box to carry all those books to and from the library. If you live in a rural area and these services are not available, take advantage of the catalogue service offered by most publishers. See pages 174–180 for publisher names and addresses.

Collect a variety of paper and art supplies. Set aside an area in your home to store these supplies. Find a space where your child can freely experiment with these art materials and have easy access to clean-up materials (water, towels, soap, etc).

Investigate possible extracurricular organizations and activities. Organizations, such as local parks and recreation departments, boys' and girls' clubs, and scouts, will offer classes and activities to meet a variety of interests. Consider sports, music, art, or dance lessons. Contact your local school district. Some public schools allow home-educated children to attend field trips, assemblies, or selected classes.

Make a list of possible field trips. Possible trips might include tide pools, museums, farms, ranches, stores, factories, theaters, and concerts.

Become familiar with your area's home-schooling requirements. Write or call your state or province. Find out what curriculum materials other home-school families are using in your area. Ask questions. Learn from others who are more experienced.

Find a support group. See page 185 for listings by state and province. These sources may be able to recommend local organizations. If you live in an isolated situation, we encourage you to stay in contact with a support group via correspondence, phone, fax, or modem.

ONE TO TWO WEEKS BEFORE "INSTRUCTION" BEGINS

Decide on a log format in which to record your child's learning. You will find an example on page 166. Feel free to develop your own or adapt the one provided, as necessary. It is important to document learning.

I think home schooling is fun because there aren't a million other kids. I get more attention. I don't have to wait very long before I get help when I need it.

—Rachel Cech, age 10

DURING AND AFTER "INSTRUCTION"

Record your child's activities. You will find that there is no way you can record all of them. Pick activities that meet state or provincial curricular guidelines.

Model learning for your child. Think out loud when you have a problem to solve so children can apply your example to their thinking and learning.

Read often in front of your child. Show by your actions that you find reading a worthwhile and enjoyable activity.

Don't panic. Many children work in bursts of energy. They focus on a project or activity for a length of time and then set it aside to pursue something new or to wait for the next burst of energy. These patterns are normal; allow them to happen.

Live your daily life and discuss your activities with your child. Invite him or her to participate whenever possible. Allow your child to become an integral part of family activities and planning.

Go to the library often; go to the bookstore too—if it's in your budget. When you go to the library, don't let your child check out just one or two books. Allow him or her to check out 30 or 40 books on a variety of subjects. You, too, can check out dozens of books. Pick books on subjects that your child generally doesn't read about. Leave them around the house for those times when he or she is in the mood for something new. Saturate your child's environment with literature.

Play a variety of games with your child. There are excellent games that indirectly teach cooperation, academic skills (math, spelling, writing), thinking skills, and problem solving. See a listing of suggested games on page 187.

Home schooling

\'hōm skü-ling\ n

1: schooling at home

2: having fun

—*Emily Windham,*

age 11

Home education requires commitment. Confidence also helps. The more experience you have in successful home schooling, the more your confidence as a home educator will grow. The interest-driven home education approach, in particular, requires a large dose of commitment and confidence.

Interest-driven education is particularly for parents who have let go of the idea that education is learning prescribed bits of information and skills. It is for parents who want to give their children the experience, confidence, and power of independent learning. It is also for parents who are able to look at a day's learning activities after the fact, record it in a learning log, and synthesize and organize the information in such a way that when called upon, they can justify their child's learning experiences in light of state or provincial requirements.

Page 101 shows a week's learning log for Emily. The parents have recorded Emily's spontaneous learning at the end of the day. They have recorded the learning by subject so they have a clear record of concepts covered. See page 166 for a blank learning log.

It should be noted that most home educators are not ready for the interest-driven approach during their first year of home schooling. Many like to warm up to it by starting with the textbook- or theme-driven approach. As their confidence and comfort level grow, they may move into a more interest-driven approach. Many parents also find they like to combine the textbook-driven, theme-driven, and interest-driven approaches—depending on the subject content, their child's interests, and their background knowledge.

LEARNING LOG

NAME: Emily Windham   GRADE: 1st   WEEK OF: Sept. 30 – Oct. 4

SUBJECT	MONDAY	TUESDAY	WEDNESDAY	THURSDAY	FRIDAY
Reading	Miss Rumphius by Barbara Cooney	Father Bear Come Home: by Else Holmelund Minarik	Frog and Toad Are Friends, by Arnold Lobel	Feel Better Ernest! by Gabrielle Vincent	Island Box, by Barbara Cooney
Language Arts	Thank-you letter	Birthday card	Granny's House: a cooperative game – Following directions, Thinking skills	Laundry basket labels	3 letters To Dad
Math	Mental Math: addition and subtraction with regrouping; multiplication facts 0 – 10. Division by 2 and 3	Play with calculator	Anno's Math Games, by Mitsumasa Anno	Anno's Math Games II	Sorting and grouping coupons
Social Studies	Service Stations: Fill It Up, by Gail Gibbons	Pioneer history and family life: Little House on the Prairie series			Life on a Fishing island: Surrounded by Sea, by Gail Gibbons
Science	Reading Rainbow: The Magic School Bus (caves)	Ranger Rick: "Rainforests" "Tell Me Why" "Scorpions"	Newton's Apple (video) whales, dinosaurs, comets, sharks	Being Born, by Sheila Kitzinger conception and birth	Prehistoric Animals, by James Shooter
Art, Music, P.E., Health, Other	Dance class Woodworking	Color chart Rainbow and Butterfly mobile	Homemade stationery	Roller skating class	Sewing

How do I teach several children at once?

Teaching several children at various grade levels requires careful planning as well as discipline on the part of both parents and children.

Lesson plans for three children on one page can be overwhelming. I photocopy each child's lesson plans on different colors of paper. That way I can quickly find each child's page.

—Joyce Ulshafer, 7 years home-school parent

Eight-year-old Sean is eagerly leaning over the kitchen table, dexterously working with math manipulatives, as his mother carefully explains the intricacies of place value. Both Sean and his mother are enjoying this shared learning experience and Sean is on the verge of understanding that "ten ones" really can be represented as "one ten" when suddenly this teachable moment is abruptly shattered. Sean's six-year-old sister, Marie, who had been happily sorting buttons according to size and shape, is now screaming at the top of her lungs while chasing three-year-old Todd through the room. Todd has emerged from his play in the backyard and has gleefully hijacked Marie's favorite stack of buttons. Marie is furious; Todd is merrily strewing buttons throughout the room and, of course, Sean is no longer remotely interested in place value.

There's just no way around it. Teaching and caring for more than one child will constantly have its challenges and its many rewards. The following suggestions will help you get started.

SCHEDULING

Develop a daily schedule that coordinates your children's lessons and activities, including activities for infants and toddlers. A sample is shown on page 103. A blank form titled Daily Schedule, Coordinating Several Children is provided on page 167.

DAILY SCHEDULE
COORDINATING SEVERAL CHILDREN

🕐	CHILD ONE James (4Th grade)	CHILD TWO Zach (2nd grade)	CHILD THREE Sarah (4 years old)
7:00-8:00 a.m.	Dress BreakfasT	Dress BreakfasT	Dress BreakfasT
8:00-9:00 a.m.	Chores IndependenT Reading *Mom explains language arTs	Chores IndependenT Reading	Chores *Mom reads To Sarah
9:00-10:00 a.m.	Language arTs	*Mom reads wiTh Zach, Teaches maTh, assigns language arTs	Plays in back yard
10:00-11:00 a.m.	*Mom discusses reading, and Teaches maTh	Language arTs	"Schoolwork" drawing, reading, blocks
LUNCH			
1:00-2:00 p.m.	Social STudies and science uniTs (done TogeTher)	Social STudies and science uniTs (done TogeTher)	Nap
2:00-3:00 p.m.	CompuTer games, biking, and free Time	CompuTer games, biking, and free Time	*Mom wiTh Sarah

COMBINING CURRICULUM CONTENT

Whenever possible have your children learn from the same materials, using a unit or thematic approach. For example, the Wongs were studying the rain forests of Brazil. They had several books about the rain forest on a variety of levels. The same content was studied by both girls, but the older child, Melinda, mastered the concepts at a deeper level and read more difficult passages to her younger sister, Jessica. Melinda, the ten-year-old, developed more sophisticated products in her follow-up assignments: a rain forest diorama, an illustrated rain forest plant and animal dictionary, and an ecology report on the plight of present-day rain forests. Six-year-old Jessica made rain forest animals from paper bags. She used the puppets to tell what she learned. Jessica also wrote and illustrated a rain forest storybook patterned after *The Great Kapok Tree*. The story was almost the same, but she changed the animals who came to the man in the forest.

Some curriculum content cannot be combined, however. Math is an example of a subject where families must individualize. Each child is given separate math assignments at appropriate levels of difficulty. Siblings can assist each other in checking work, drilling with flash cards, and playing math games, but these activities must be at their own levels.

If your children are one or two years apart, it is fairly easy to combine some of the curriculum content, but if you have a first grader and an eighth grader, it will be much more difficult to combine curriculum content.

If you individualize only math and reading, the form titled Lesson Plans for Two Children on page 172 might assist you.

Record all activities that your children will do together in the top portion. List individual assignments in the lower portion. Make extra copies of the blank form on page 172 if you have more than two school-age children.

If your children are one or two years apart, it is fairly easy to combine some of the curriculum content.

LESSON PLANS FOR TWO CHILDREN

STUDENTS: Matt Smith | Elizabeth Smith

DATES: October 6 - 10

TOGETHER:

Monday	**Language Arts:** compose Haiku about the sea
	Social Studies: map activity — draw world map and trace migration of humpback whales
Tuesday	**Language Arts:** listen to tape with sea sounds; write creative story based on tape
	Art: paint watercolor to illustrate story
Wednesday	**Language Arts:** written summary of Ranger Rick article
	Science: read and discuss Ranger Rick article on reef fish
Thursday	**Language Arts:** mini oral report about one sea animal
	Science: classification of marine life
Friday	**Field Trip:** Marine Institute (take pictures for next week's writing)

	Name: Elizabeth Grade: 3	**Name:** Matt Grade: 5
Monday Math: Indep. Reading: Other:	Pages 34-35 (Modern Curriculum Press) Peter The Friendly Whale	Lesson 18 (John Saxon) Island of the Blue Dolphins Research paper (dolphins): note cards
Tuesday Math: Indep. Reading: Other:	Pages 36-37 Peter The Friendly Whale	Lesson 19 Island of the Blue Dolphins Research paper: note cards
Wednesday Math: Indep. Reading: Other:	Pages 38-39 The Ocean Floor	Lesson 20 Island of the Blue Dolphins Journal entry
Thursday Math: Indep. Reading: Other:	Pages 40-41 The Ocean Floor	Lesson 21 Island of the Blue Dolphins Guitar lesson
Friday Math: Indep. Reading: Other:	Pages 42-43 Amazing Sea Facts	Test Island of the Blue Dolphins

ORGANIZING TEACHING SPACE

Organize your teaching space to maximize your availability. Many mothers of primary children find it helpful to organize their children's desks or tables so they can rotate between them. This allows the parent to work with one child while being available to answer a quick question from another child. If you have toddlers or preschoolers, you may want to allocate a special workplace for them in or near your working area. Preschoolers can feel part of the program if they are provided activities at their own level. While this arrangement often works well for 15 to 20 minutes, most mothers of toddlers schedule tasks requiring the most concentration or quiet for their K–8 children at their toddler's nap time.

SIBLING ASSISTANCE

Enlist your older children to help with younger ones. Older children can answer questions, explain directions, or teach concepts with which they are already familiar. Teaching reinforces the older sibling's learning as well as develops an awareness of family needs and responsibility. Younger children are often receptive and enthusiastic about information presented or reviewed by an admired big brother or sister.

FLEXIBLE SCHEDULING

Plan a flexible year-round schedule. Even with the help of a supportive spouse and well-trained children, chances are good that the more children you have, the harder you will work and the more breaks your family will need. Many large families use a modified year-round schedule and take a week off every six weeks with a month off in the summer. Other families accomplish their academic work in four days, leaving Friday free for field trips and family projects.

OTHER-CENTEREDNESS

Remember, you, your children, and your home-school experience will not be perfect. Take advantage of those less-than-perfect moments to help your children learn to listen to each other and to discuss their conflicts. As children learn to openly communicate, they learn to consider the needs and views of others, including their parents. Children will soon realize that the close proximity they share in the intimacy of their home dramatically compounds the effects of each person's actions. Consistent guidance about being considerate of each other's needs is a priceless, life-long gift that will serve your child well both now and in the future.

My husband and I have learned that loving and consistent discipline is a must.

—Holly Preston, 2 years home-school parent

How do I motivate my child to do the work?

At some point in time, every teacher, whether teaching a class of thirty or a single student at home, is challenged to motivate children to do their schoolwork.

Don't whine. You need to do the work anyway, so it's best to cooperate with your mom.

—Daniel Wevodau, age 9

As one home-school mom said, *The propensity to piddle has got to be one of the most innate of all childhood characteristics.* Fortunately, there are many strategies available to you as a home educator that will assist you when your child is not interested in or chooses not to do his or her schoolwork.

DETERMINE WHO IS RESPONSIBLE FOR LEARNING

When planning a lesson that is difficult or "boring" for your child, seek to transfer the responsibility of the learning from you, the teacher, to your child, the learner. This principle is dubbed *Locus of Control* by educational researchers. Research shows us that involvement or responsibility is one of the key factors involved in motivation. A student who believes that someone else is responsible for his or her learning is defensive and insecure and often resists or complains about assignments. Therefore, when dealing with subjects that your child views as not important, difficult, or routine; the first step is to increase his or her sense of control over the learning process.

To help children feel responsible for learning, try the following:

• Encourage your child to plan and set goals for learning as well as time frames for accomplishing the work. A student who is involved in the planning process receives a concrete sense of his or her own participation in the act of learning.

Many parents have found that their child has benefited from completing a daily goal sheet. A sample goal sheet is shown on page 106. A blank reproducible form can be found on page 173.

• Encourage your child to use self-evaluation procedures. The easiest way to do this is to determine together ahead of time the standards you will be using to evaluate your child's work. Record these standards and have your child evaluate his or her work in light of predetermined standards. Here is an example of oral reading and editorial inspection standards. A blank form is on page 168.

• Encourage your child to use a log or graph to record progress. This consistent visual image helps reinforce progress.

• Help your child analyze his or her strengths and abilities and choose learning tasks appropriate to these areas. For example, if your child has a talent for summarizing and writing clearly, he or she would probably be successful in writing a news article or conducting a "live" news report. Help your child choose tailor-made assignments that tap into his or her strengths and empower him or her to learn.

• Help your child analyze potential blocks to progress in their learning. For example, *You have wonderful creative ideas but it's difficult for you to summarize your thoughts and record them on paper. Let's work on this together.* Such feedback and assistance helps alleviate your child's sense of being overwhelmed by a difficult task and prepares your child for further frustration or slower progress.

• Discuss with your older children college and career choices and steps to reach long-term goals. Looking ahead give older children a sense of direction in their schooling.

• Celebrate with your child when he or she accomplishes a goal. Encourage your child to savor learning successes.

Have a great attitude about your school work and have fun with it. Learn things in a way that makes it interesting and fun.
—Marykate Bell, age 14

ORAL READING STANDARDS

1. I spoke up loudly enough for all to hear.
2. I pronounced my words clearly.
3. I held by head so that the audience could see my face.
4. I looked at the audience as often as I could without losing my place.
5. I read in word groups instead of word by word.
6. When reading informational material, I read it slowly and clearly the way the author would talk.
7. When reading conversations, I read the lines as the characters would have said them.

| | YES | NO | BETTER |

My goal for next time:

EDITORIAL INSPECTION STANDARDS

The last steps in successful writing are editing and proofreading. Use the editorial tips listed below to help you decide if your work is complete.

Structure
1. Is the main idea clearly stated in the topic sentence?
2. Do the sentences that follow the topic sentence give supporting details?
3. Does each new paragraph begin the topic sentence?

Mechanics
4. Do all the sentences express a complete idea?
5. Is the first word of each paragraph indented?
6. Does each sentence and each proper noun begin with a capital letter?
7. Did I check spelling?
8. Does each sentence have the correct punctuation mark?

| | Yes | No |

My goal for next time:

CONSIDER USING EXTRINSIC MOTIVATION

When dealing with difficult or routine subjects, the use of extrinsic reinforcement (goodies, rewards, or privileges) can be successful in "spicing things up" and motivating your child. Consider the following points:

• Use extrinsic rewards *only when necessary.* They should be just powerful enough to motivate and phased out when intrinsic reinforcement becomes evident. For example, if your child loves to read, he or she is already experiencing the intrinsic value of reading. It is not necessary (and would be unwise) to extrinsically reward your child for reading. If, however, the same child resists memorizing the multiplication facts, an extrinsic reward might just provide the needed motivation to accomplish this task. Reality tells us that there will be some tasks for which a child may never feel intrinsically motivated.

• If you choose to use extrinsic motivation, remember to reinforce even small improvements in learning and motivation. Avoid demanding too much before providing motivation.

• Be sure you offer the positive reinforcement your child wants. Brainstorm a list of rewards with your child. Consider extra privileges, a favorite food treat, stickers, a special outing, or the elimination of a chore or assignment.

Jenni Key, a home-school parent with nine years of experience, describes her ticket system of extrinsic reward: *I've gotten heaps of mileage out of a roll of tickets like the ones used at a carnival. My kids get a ticket just for showing up at "school," for homework assignments completed, for extra credit work. We have ticket drawings frequently for candy or other small prizes, or they can accumulate tickets to trade in for a soda, an ice-cream cone, or video rental. They're quick to remind me when it's "ticket time!"*

EMPHASIZE THE INTERESTS OF YOUR CHILD

This strategy acknowledges that your child is not a passive recipient of knowledge. When material is interesting to your child, he or she actively participates in the learning process. Active and enthusiastic participation ensures genuine, long-term, meaningful, and pleasurable learning. Unfortunately, there is not a step-by-step recipe for implementing this approach. The process is different for each child. As a home-education parent, however, you can structure the academic environment in a manner that capitalizes on the interests of your child, and increases the likelihood that meaningful learning will occur. Keep these points in mind:

• Place less emphasis on prepackaged materials and textbook-driven schooling. Many children thrive in a learning environment in which they can move about and explore topics of interest to them. Too much emphasis on textbooks and worksheets tends to dampen some children's interest in learning.

• Place more emphasis on the interests of your child. Use the advantages of home education to take time to pursue your child's interests and inspirations. When he or she freely selects a book, topic, or activity, interest is a given. Questions of motivation, incentives, and rewards become irrelevant. The learning is its own incentive and the knowledge gained is its own reward. Granted, such pursuits end up looking very different from "regular" school work, but you will be working a small miracle. You will be helping your child make the transition from having to learn to wanting to learn.

Student Tip: Get all your work done on time and stay organized. Do your best at everything and don't give up—even when it's hard.

—Jocilynn Endresen, age 13

The Encarnacion Family

Gerry, Bambi

Gabriel (14)

Michelle (13)

Joel (11)

—*9 Years*

Home Schooling

With three children in sixth, seventh, and eighth grades, I have many opportunities to check their understanding of lessons by having them teach each other concepts. When a child can explain a lesson to a sibling and have it be clearly understood by his or her "student," then he or she has successfully grasped the idea. We apply new math skills through practical applications such as cooking. We measure ingredients, follow directions, and cut recipes in half to test knowledge of fractions. I also make statements during the day that are wrong in concept to see if the children catch it. They love this because they think they've caught Mom making a mistake when in reality, it's more of a fun form of a quiz. Of course, the yearly tests and written quizzes are time-tested ways to know where children stand academically—but it is when they can apply the concepts to real life that you know the concepts are well-ingrained. —Bambi Bonus-Encarnacion, home-school mom

Evaluation

- How do I know if my child is learning?

- What factors should I consider if my child isn't reading as well as other children?

- How do home-educated children compare academically with other children?

- What factors should I consider when determining how long to home school?

- How well do children adjust to the transition from a home-school setting to a traditional school setting?

- What types of common learning difficulties might my child encounter?

- What if my child has learning disabilities?

How do I know if my child is learning?

You will know if your child is learning because as a home-school parent, you will receive immediate feedback. In addition, informal and formal tests will give you specific feedback.

IMMEDIATE FEEDBACK

Clearly, one of the major advantages of home education is that it allows for *immediate* feedback. Educational researchers tell us that motivation to learn, to grow, and to change is significantly enhanced if feedback (what was done right and wrong) is provided immediately after an assignment is given. The longer a child or adult has to wait for feedback, the less motivated he or she is to correct mistakes and learn new information.

During the course of any one home-school lesson a child's misconception can be quickly corrected, a spark of interest can be ignited, and an idea can be developed and explored. Questions can be asked, assignments checked, and corrections made all within the framework of the lesson.

By far, the most valuable assessment tools that you possess as a home educator are *observation* and *discussion*. However, as a child grows and develops, he or she completes an ever-increasing amount of independent work at an ever-increasing difficulty level. At this point, informal, diagnostic, and standardized tests become useful tools. These tests help gauge mastery of material as well as assess overall performance.

Being able to catch the mistake as they make it is a great added value to teaching at home.

—Tammy Cahill, 5 years home-school parent

INFORMAL TESTS

After a unit or concept is taught, an informal test may follow. This type of informal test is designed to see if your child understands the material. The informal test might be in the textbook you are using (e.g., an end-of-the-unit test or end-of-the-chapter quiz), or it might be a test you have written yourself. For example, when the Jones family completed their tide pool unit, Mrs. Jones wrote a test which included true/false, multiple choice, and essay questions about the flora and fauna of tide pools. She developed this informal test to see if her third- and fifth-grade children had mastered the key concepts in the unit. As a child gets older, many parents begin to use informal tests to help assess learning and to help their children prepare for more formalized testing.

Informal tests are useful tools for assessing learning because they assess concepts that were specifically covered. Informal tests can also serve as documentation of learning in the event that your state or province requires grades or documentation of progress. Tests should not be given for the sake of giving tests or because "that's the way it's always been done." Tests should be given for a purpose—to satisfy a goal of the parent or to meet a requirement of the state, province, or territory.

DIAGNOSTIC TESTS

Diagnostic tests are published tests that are useful tools in determining particular strengths and weaknesses in subject areas. Major content areas are broken down into subskills with grade-level equivalents determined for each subskill. Examples of diagnostic tests include: Woodcock Reading Battery, Key Math Diagnostic Arithmetic Test, Diagnostic Achievement Battery, and the Gessel Development Test. Results of diagnostic tests are specific and can therefore be useful in targeting areas that need instruction. For example, Sally, age eight, was struggling to progress in reading. Mrs. Plaugher, Sally's mother, took her to a home-school consultant and requested diagnostic testing. The specialist gave Sally the Woodcock Reading Battery and found that Sally's word attack skills were strong while her comprehension skills were weak. Mrs. Plaugher and the specialist together developed a program to improve Sally's reading comprehension skills.

Tests should be given for a purpose—to satisfy a goal of the parent or to meet a requirement of the state, province, or territory.

It is not always easy to find a qualified person to administer diagnostic tests. Because they are administered individually, the fee is usually higher than fees paid for traditional standardized tests. However, because the information gained is practical and specific, many parents find it worth the time and money. Call your Department or Ministry of Education, local home-school educational agency, local school or district office, testing service, or tutoring service to get names of people who are qualified to administer diagnostic tests to your child.

STANDARDIZED TESTS

Standardized tests are generally administered in public and private schools once a year. Examples of commonly used standardized tests include: the Comprehensive Tests of Basic Skills (CTBS), Iowa Test of Basic Skills, Stanford Achievement Test, and the Metropolitan Achievement Test. A standardized test is a test that is given to a group of students under the same or "standardized" conditions.

Norms have been established for standardized tests so that the test results will tell you how your child performs in relationship to other children the same age who have taken the same test, following the same guidelines. For example, Gary, a seventh grader, received

a score of 7.5 in math computation on the Stanford Achievement Test. This meant that Gary correctly answered the same number of questions as was typical of students in the norming group that were in their fifth month of seventh grade. However, Gary also received a 5.1 in reading comprehension. This meant that Gary's reading comprehension score was typical of the average fifth grader in the norming group in his or her first month of fifth grade. Gary's scores indicated he is doing fine in math but that he did not score in the normal range for his age group in reading. Mr. and Mrs. Marshall adjusted their home-schooling program to reflect increased time on reading development.

Many home-school programs include standardized testing as part of the services they provide. If you are home schooling independently, many public schools will agree to test your child along with their students. With this arrangement, your child comes to school on testing days and takes the test with the appropriate grade-level class. This service is usually free.

There are many materials that have been developed to help children do well on standardized tests. Use of these materials is especially helpful if your child is not accustomed to taking tests or becomes nervous in testing situations. See pages 186 for specific information.

A WORD OF CAUTION

Used properly, tests are a tool to *assist* parents in making appropriate educational choices; however, tests provide only *one* way to assess a child's learning. A test score should *never* be the single piece of information used in making decisions about your child's education. The reason for this is two-fold:

1) There is room for error in test-making and test-taking. A student who is insecure or unsure about test directions—or

perhaps tired, hungry, or distracted—will receive a score that is an inaccurate reflection of his or her abilities.

2) There is not a test on the market today that provides a complete picture of a student's knowledge, creativity, motivation, and abilities.

As you develop the art of "kid watching," you will learn much about your child and what he or she does or doesn't know. Think carefully about the type of evaluation that will be most appropriate for your child. Ideally any form of testing should be a tool to help you refine your teaching and to identify areas of strengths and/or weaknesses in your child's learning.

There is not a test on the market today that provides a complete picture of a student's knowledge, creativity, motivation, and abilities.

What factors should I consider if my child isn't reading as well as other children?

Children the same age or in the same grade should not be expected to read at the same ability level any more than they would be expected to run at the same speed or have the same batting average.

DEVELOPMENTAL SCHEDULES

Children develop at different rates. This is as true of intellectual development as it is for physical and emotional development. Not all children learn to walk at one, talk at two, or read at six. To expect a child to master a skill for which he or she might be developmentally unready can create undue stress. A warm, nurturing environment where a child is allowed to acquire skills following his or her *own* developmental schedule is what most children need.

For example, one parent thought his child had dyslexia (a disturbance of the ability to read) because he kept reversing b's and d's in his reading and writing. This is a frequent phenomenon that occurs with children up to third grade. These reversals occur because some children are still developing their directionality. Be careful to consider your child's *individual* developmental clock—it may be that your child is developing at a different rate than a peer whom you've observed. A good rule of thumb is: don't compare. Accept your children just as they are, and take pleasure in providing a nurturing environment in which they can develop at their own rate. However, if testing indicates that your child is developing at a disparate rate to the norm (two or more years behind in a given subject area), it would be wise to give this area immediate attention.

LINGUISTIC INCLINATION

Another reason your child may be developing at a different rate in reading than other children of his or her age is that children have varying degrees of linguistic intelligence. If your child starts reading early, reads well, and reads voraciously, then he or she is linguistically inclined. Give thanks! These children learn to read regardless of how they are taught. If your child starts reading late, doesn't read well, and prefers not to read, then your child is probably not linguistically inclined. Does this mean that he or she will never learn to read? Of course not. Your child will learn to read in his or her own time. Your role is to provide the most nurturing atmosphere possible and the most appropriate guidance possible, so that your child can do his or her

> *A warm, nurturing environment in which a child is allowed to acquire skills following his or her **own** developmental schedule is what most children need.*

best. You also may have to work harder in this area. You may need to comb the libraries for books of the appropriate level and of interest to your child. You will also want books with appropriate size print, supporting illustrations, and appropriate amounts of text to help ensure successful early reading experiences.

If your child learns to read later than your neighbor's child who is the same age, it is *not* a poor reflection on your parenting abilities, your teaching abilities, or your child's intelligence. Most children, unless there is a serious learning problem, will learn to read according to their own developmental timetable.

SELECTING A READING PROGRAM

Literature-based or skill-based, phonics or sight vocabulary, basal or whole language—which reading program is best for your child? No one reading program works for every child. Christy Cech, who has home schooled for the last five years, found this to be true with her daughters—*Teaching my two daughters to read proved to be an insightful experience for me. I used similar methods with both girls, however, reading didn't click for my oldest until shortly before third grade. In contrast, my middle daughter was a fluent reader by first grade. Both girls are now excellent readers. I'm thankful I was able to allow each of them to mature at their own rate without the pressure of peer comparison. I now look forward to teaching my youngest to read.*

Since no one program works every time, examination of the child's needs must precede the program and the instructional approach. Reading instruction is facilitated when the program is matched with individual learning styles. For example, if your child's preferred learning modality is visual or kinesthetic, a phonics based program could be a struggle. The reason for this, of course, would be that you would be asking your child to learn to read using his or her weakest modality, auditory. However, you could adapt the phonics approach (primarily auditory) by always keeping a visual cue in front of your child (e.g., the letter with an animal) when introducing phonics concepts. The visual cues would serve as memory tools for your child and would tap into his or her strongest learning modality. If you introduce the phonics concept within the context of a literature book (more of a whole language approach), the learning setting would become even stronger. The freedom to match a program to your child's learning style is one of the unique advantages of home education.

The following pages highlight ten steps to reading success for emerging and developing readers.

Examination of the child's needs must precede the program and the instructional approach.

TEN STEPS TO READING SUCCESS

1. Read aloud.
This is the basic requirement. You read to your child and your child reads to you and other family members. Even older children benefit from listening to a more experienced reader.

2. Read for pleasure.
Let your child read for fun about topics that are of interest to him or her. If your child reads primarily to complete worksheets, take tests, or write book reports, he or she may gain a negative impression of reading.

3. Read often.
Frequency improves fluency.

4. Read different kinds of books.
Variety is essential for most children. Check out a couple of dozen library books instead of three or four. When your child loses interest in one subject or book (and he or she will), have an assortment of alternative books available to fill the curiosity gap.

I like home schooling because I can read what and when I want to.

—Amy Windham, age 8

5. Allow your child to read easy books.
Everything your child reads need not be a challenge. Children benefit from reading what adults consider "easy" materials. A book in the hand is worth two on the shelf.

6. Allow your child to make reading errors.
Beginning and developing readers are going to make mistakes, just as beginning walkers and beginning talkers make mistakes. It is an important part of the learning process. We generally consider the blunders made by young children learning to walk and talk as cute or amusing. However, when children learning to read make errors, we wonder about learning disabilities and consult specialists. Making mistakes is a part of any learning process. Constantly spotlighting errors can dim the light of enthusiasm for a beginning reader of any age.

7. Reread books.
Rereading books builds confidence, improves fluency, aids comprehension, and heightens enjoyment. Memorizing stories they hear again and again is the first step to reading for many children.

8. **Discuss the books you have read.**

   Informal discussion can promote understanding and is a more appropriate instructional strategy than worksheets for most children.

9. **Be seen reading, rereading, and discussing books.**

   If your child sees you reading frequently, he or she learns by your actions that reading is a valued activity. Your example can provide added incentive for beginning and developing readers.

10. **Be patient.**

    Children learn at different rates. There is no set timetable. A child who is not linguistically inclined will take longer to learn to read. This is due to the *type* of intelligence, not the amount of intelligence.

For more information helpful to beginning and developing readers, read Jim Trelease's *Read-Aloud Handbook for Parents*.

Making mistakes is a part of any learning process. Constantly spotlighting errors can dim the light of enthusiasm for a beginning reader of any age.

How do home-educated children compare academically with other children?

Studies indicate that home-educated children, as a group, perform academically at least as well as or better than their classroom counterparts.

80TH PERCENTILE

In 1990, a major national report was released by the National Home Education Research Institute which studied the test results for close to 1500 home-educated children (*Home School Court Report*. The Home School Legal Defense Association: December 1990). The average scores for these children were at or above the 80th percentile in all categories. The categories included reading, listening, language, math, science, and social studies. The major standardized tests used included the California Achievement Test, the Iowa Test of Basic Skills, and the Stanford Achievement Test (SAT). An 80th percentile score means that the students scored better than or equal to 80 percent of the students used to norm that particular level of the test. This study supports the claim that home-educated children, as a group, perform academically at least as well or better than their counterparts in traditional classrooms.

Other sources reporting the success of home schooling include:

> *The average home-schooled students register between the 65th and 80th percentiles.*

Time: "While the national average (on standardized tests) is in the 50th percentile, the average home-schooled students register between the 65th and 80th percentiles." (Gibbs, Nancy. "Home Sweet School." *Time,* October 31, 1994, p. 63.)

Teachers College Record: Educational research conducted by the Hewitt Research Foundation found that performance scores in the 75th to 95th percentile are common for home-schooled children. The study included several thousand home-schooled children across the United States. Many of the parents spent no more than an hour or two a day teaching their children. (Moore, Raymond. "Research and Common Sense: Therapies for Our Home and Schools." *Teachers College Record,* Columbia University, Vol. 84, No. 2, 1982, p. 372.)

Phi Delta Kappa: This study found that home-schooled children received higher scores on standardized achievement tests than did their peers in Los Angeles public schools. (Weaver, Roy et. al. "Home Tutorials vs. Public Schools in Los Angeles." *Phi Delta Kappa,* December 1980, pp. 254-255.)

Home Education Magazine: In South Dakota, home-schooled fourth graders received the highest SAT scores in the state. The tests are required annually. Seventy-four percent of the home-schooled fourth graders tested have never attended public or private school. (*Home Education Magazine,* Vol. 11, No. 2, March–April 1994, p. 49.)

OUR EXPERIENCE

Both authors have worked for a major public school independent study program designed to assist home-educating families. This program is run by the Orange County Department of Education in Southern California. It is the largest public independent study program in the state of California. Current enrollment is over 870 students. Family situations and socioeconomic levels are diverse.

Once a year the program offers optional standardized testing (Comprehensive Test of Basic Skills—CTBS) to its families. The majority of the children are tested. Testing occurs at the site offices sponsored by the County Department of Education. The testing environment is formal, and the tests are administered and proctored by credentialed teachers. All security measures are followed to insure valid test results. The home-school students' average test scores are higher than the national norm year after year. Scores indicate that home-educated children are learning essential concepts as defined by standardized testing.

The home-school students' average test scores are higher than the national norm year after year.

What factors should I consider when determining how long to home school?

There is not an ideal, predetermined time for a child to make the transition from home education to a more traditional classroom setting. However, there are several key factors to consider when making the right choice for your family.

INITIAL REASONS

Evaluate your initial reasons for home schooling. This evaluation will undoubtedly serve as the most accurate measure of when or if your child should enter school. For example, David's parents began home schooling him when he was five years old. Although David was bright and already had a basic understanding of reading and math concepts, his parents wanted to provide him with additional time at home to learn and grow before placing him in a large-group setting. After two years of home education, David was a confident, outgoing seven-year-old who loved learning. His parents felt that their initial goals for David had been met and placed him in a second-grade classroom where he thrived both academically and socially.

The Andersons made the decision to home school when their daughters had just completed third and fourth grades. The girls enjoyed school and did well academically; however, they repeatedly complained of long days and wasted time while they studied "stuff we already know." The girls were both talented musically and were involved in music lessons, choir practices, and musical productions. The Andersons hoped that home schooling would enable their daughters to progress at their own rate while providing additional time for each to pursue her interest and talent in music.

The decision to continue home schooling should always be made in light of how it affects the entire family.

After a trial year of home schooling, the Andersons were convinced that the home-school setting maximized learning for their daughters and allowed them more time to pursue musical interests. The Andersons' previously hectic lifestyle is now more relaxed; they plan to continue home schooling for several more years.

FAMILY NEEDS

The decision to continue home schooling should always be made in light of how it affects the entire family. Sometimes pressing family emergencies make it difficult, if not impossible, to continue home schooling. Parents often make the decision to terminate home schooling as other pressing family needs emerge. Perhaps an ailing grandparent is moving in who requires continual care, or perhaps it has become imperative for a parent to work outside the home and supplement the family income. At other times, the situation is not as drastic but still warrants serious consideration. Perhaps Mom feels she is not able to adequately provide for the care and nurturing of her infant and toddler while home schooling her first and third graders. Or, maybe Dad has taken a new job and is now traveling extensively, making him unable to assist with schooling and household chores.

YOUR CHILD'S INTERESTS AND DESIRES

Evaluate your child's interests and desires. Children often have strong feelings about whether or not they want to continue home schooling. Of course, you are the parent and you will ultimately make the decision based on your child's best interests. However, at its best, home schooling is a learning partnership between parent and child. Certainly the desires and interests of your child should be given strong consideration. And, it is often prudent to listen to the counsel of trusted family members, friends, and professionals who know you and your child well and have your child's best interest in mind.

The desires and interests of your child should be given strong consideration.

The Watson family clearly illustrates the importance of considering your child's interests and desires. The Watsons began home schooling 18 years ago when their oldest son, Ted, was five. When Ted reached fifth grade, he made it clear that he wanted to "go to school" and be "taught by a real teacher." His parents realized how strongly Ted felt and enrolled him in the local public school. Ted had some initial adjustments to make but was soon happy and doing well. Ted has just graduated from high school with a 3.9 grade-point average and will be enrolling in a university near his home.

Since entering school at fifth grade was so successful for Ted, his parents assumed that his younger sister Emily would also follow this pattern. However, as fifth grade approached, Emily was steadfast in her desire to continue home education. She was involved in an active home-school support group, the 4H club, and the church youth group. Since Emily was thriving academically as well as socially, her parents decided to honor her request and continued to home school her.

Emily will soon enter the eighth grade at home. She is an avid reader and has had several poems published in children's magazines. She is computer literate, with great keyboard skills, so she can make spending money by typing Ted's papers for him. Emily hopes her parents will continue to home school her throughout high school.

By carefully weighing their children's input, the Watsons have provided an excellent, but different, educational experience for both of their children.

Janie Anderson, a home-school parent with nine years of experience, underscores the importance of accommodating the needs and desires of each individual child—*Be flexible to change your methods as your needs change with each child. Last year I had one child in*

home school, one in public school, one in private school, and one preschool age. Though the Anderson's situation is unusual, it does point out that taking advantage of different educational settings may be the way to accommodate the individual needs within your family.

Gabriel Encarnacion, an eighth grader who has been home schooled the last nine years, describes the thoughts that went into his decision to change educational settings—*Before making the decision to go into public school, I asked myself a few questions: Am I able to follow through on my responsibilities and complete my work diligently? Am I able to get along with new people and yet not be swayed by peer pressure? Will*

this move introduce me to higher academic and extra-curricular challenges? Do I have the support of the other members of my family? Only when these questions were answered positively did I decide to enter public school.*

COMMITMENT AND MOTIVATION

Evaluate your commitment to home schooling. Home schooling, even with the brightest children, takes a lot of work. An important factor to consider is your desire and motivation to continue. Before listing "burnout" at the top of your "Ten Reasons to Quit Home Schooling" list, read the section titled *How do I avoid burnout?* on pages 146–151. There is hope for the weary!

Before making the decision to go into public school, I asked myself a few questions: Am I able to follow through on my responsibilities and complete my work diligently? Am I able to get along with new people and yet not be swayed by peer pressure?

—Gabriel Encarnacion, age 14

How well do children adjust to the transition from a home-school setting to a traditional school setting?

Although experiences vary widely, most home-educated children face little serious difficulty when they enter or reenter school, whether at the elementary, high school, or college level.

If you are positive about the transition, your child most likely will be also.

A few of the factors which affect how a child adjusts to a transition from home school to a traditional school setting include: the quality and length of your child's home-education experience; the quality of the school to which your child is entering or returning; the vision, commitment, and understanding of the teachers to whom you are entrusting your child; your understanding of and commitment to the traditional school setting; and your child's desire to make the transition. Cynthia M. Hachey, a home-school mom with five years of experience, describes how their family made the transition with their son, Michael—*I home schooled my son Michael for four years from kindergarten to third grade. These were wonderful, growing years for Michael and our family. In fourth grade Michael expressed a desire to go to our local public school. I struggled with this decision, but after placing Michael in school and seeing how well he is doing, I realized that our home-school experience had not been a failure because it had ended but rather, it was a success, having fostered a secure, independent learner.*

THE COLFAX'S

The Colfax's are probably the most well-known home-education family. In their book *Homeschooling for Excellence*, David and Micki Colfax describe their experiences home educating their four sons in a remote Northern California farm setting. The boys were home educated through high school. All four sons successfully entered the school system at the college level. Grant Colfax, the oldest son, was named a Fulbright Scholar and attended Harvard Medical School. Drew Colfax was awarded a Rockefeller Scholarship and is working toward a Ph.D. at the University of Michigan. Drew also received a National Science Foundation Fellowship. Reed Colfax attends Yale Law School. Garth, the youngest son, attends a local junior college and works with developmentally disadvantaged youth. True, the Colfax's are not representative of all home-educated children. But if higher education is the litmus test, their experiences provide an example of the success that can be attained.

OTHER SUCCESS STORIES

Home Education Magazine is an informative and helpful publication that offers home-education parents thoughtful and non-extremist support (see page 190). Each issue includes information on networking and support groups; feature articles on home-education issues; and political analysis, commentaries, and opinions about proposed bills and other actions affecting home educators. There is also a section called "News Watch" by Linda Dobson that pulls together home-education related newspaper and magazine articles, radio interviews, and TV news stories from around the country. Every issue contains at least one story about colleges that accept or actively recruit home-educated students, home-educated children who compete successfully in local and state academic competitions, or home-educated children acquiring college degrees years ahead of their age peers. Some of these children reenter school and perform outstanding feats of academic achievement.

IT'S UP TO YOU

If a child is doing well academically in a home-education setting, there is little reason to doubt that he or she will also do well in a traditional school setting.

Conversely, if a home-educated child is not doing well academically, then he or she may not do any better in school where individualization is more difficult. There will be exceptions in both cases. There also may be other factors, such as special learning needs and socialization that must also be considered in each child's case.

The reality is that the quality of your child's home-education experience and the quality of his or her transition to a traditional school setting is primarily in your hands. If you choose to transition to a traditional school setting, then it is important to be supportive of that setting. Volunteer in your child's classroom; assist the classroom teacher; become active in parent/teacher organizations. If you are positive about the transition, your child most likely will be also.

If a child is doing well academically in a home-education setting, there is little reason to doubt that he or she will also do well in a traditional school setting.

What types of common learning difficulties might my child encounter?

Every child, whether formally schooled or home schooled, will have difficulty grasping, applying, or remembering a new idea or skill at some point in his or her education.

Many home-school parents identify common problems with which their children struggle academically. Typical areas of concern include: reading fluency, reading comprehension, spelling, written expression, and the multiplication tables. There are many simple strategies for remedying these common difficulties. We will discuss a few of these problems as well as some simple strategies for remediation.

Many home-school parents identify common problems with which their children struggle academically.

READING FLUENCY

When a fluent reader reads aloud, the text flows. A beginning or developing reader, however, will read with many pauses and hesitations. This choppiness in oral reading is normal for the beginning reader. What is usually of concern to parents is when an older child exhibits this type of oral reading behavior. There are no quick solutions—your child will develop at his or her own rate. There are things you can do, however, to help your child's reading development. The Ten Steps to Reading Success found on pages 118–119 is a good place to start.

The importance of reading to your child, reading in front of your child, and surrounding your child with reading material cannot be overemphasized. It might also help to keep in mind that oral reading is not the same as silent reading. For some children, oral reading is a form of acting. There is an audience of critics ready to point out any errors made. The child's nervousness in oral reading may be analogous to an actor's stage fright. You can help by *not* correcting every oral reading mistake your child makes. Another way to improve fluency and reduce stress is to tell your child the pronunciation of a difficult word rather than interrupting the flow of the story to have him or her sound out a word.

READING COMPREHENSION

Some children have difficulty understanding or remembering what they have read because the material is too difficult or of little interest or relevancy to them. Besides adjusting for difficulty or interest, there are several approaches a parent can take to improve reading comprehension. One approach is to teach a child to visualize what he or she is reading. Ask questions like — *How do you picture the main character? What kind of clothes is he wearing? What kinds of details do you imagine in this scene?* In this way a child will learn to "see" the story, not just the words.

Another way to improve reading comprehension is to help a child increase his or her silent reading rate. Most of us read silently as if we were reading orally word by word. For some children, this interferes with comprehension because they are reading too slowly to put together the pieces of the main idea. They focus too much energy and attention on the individual words and miss the overall picture. The child mistakenly equates reading with *saying* the words rather than understanding and processing the *meaning* of the words.

Improving reading rate often improves reading comprehension, however, it is usually best to wait until the child is reading at a fourth-grade level before beginning to address reading rate. By this time, most children have mastered basic word attack skills and are more than ready to learn to read in lines and phrases rather than word by word. As they learn to read groups of words, they are able to process meaning at an increased rate.

The importance of reading to your child, reading in front of your child, and surrounding your child with reading material cannot be overemphasized.

SPELLING

It is common for home-schooling parents, as well as classroom teachers, to despair over children's spelling habits. Children who are successful on Friday's spelling tests do not always apply their knowledge of the weekly spelling lists when writing stories or reports. Many experienced home educators and classroom teachers de-emphasize weekly spelling lists and concentrate more on spelling in context. For beginning and developing writers, they place more emphasis on the content and clarity of the writing than on the mechanics and conventions (capitalization, punctuation, and spelling).

The use of personal spelling journals is a practical alternative to spelling lists. The parent marks the spelling mistakes made in writing assignments. The correct spelling of these words is then listed in the journal. The child uses the journal as an individualized dictionary. The spelling journal has two advantages. First, rote memorization is de-emphasized. Second, the child learns to spell words that are a part of his or her speaking vocabulary.

Some parents take a high-tech approach to spelling problems by purchasing small electronic spellers or by teaching a child to use a word processor that offers a spell-check program. Electronic gadgets, however, aren't perfect when it comes to spelling in context. Children still must learn when to use *there, their,* or *they're.*

MATH FACTS

Attempting to teach a child the basic math facts can sometimes be an exercise in frustration. The traditional approaches involve rote memory, written and oral repetition, and timed drills. These methods do not work for every child. It is common for a child to demonstrate mastery over the facts one day and seem to forget the same facts the next day.

Children need to understand a math concept before they can retain it. Use manipulatives (beans, chips, candy, etc.) to demonstrate concepts. For example, three groups of four items and four groups of three items both equal twelve. Visual demonstrations make it easier for most children to learn that $3 \times 4 = 12$. Math games are an inviting way to help children internalize math facts. Most children will gladly learn math computation skills in order to play a game. The skills become incidental to the game instead of the subject of repetitive drills and worksheets. See page 187 for a list of math games.

HOME SCHOOLING CAN HELP

We have just discussed a few of the academic challenges you and your children may encounter during your years of home schooling. Many problems like these are reduced when new skills and ideas are presented in ways that children find interesting. An understanding and appreciation of how new concepts and skills apply to their lives and the lives of their family and friends will help children master new material. Matching your teaching strategies, activities, and materials to your child's learning style will also eliminate or lessen some of the common learning problems you may encounter.

As we have stated before, there are several advantages to home schooling when it comes to remedying common learning difficulties. One advantage is the freedom to individualize your child's academic program. When you individualize, you can teach your child what he or she needs when he or she needs it. Another advantage is the flexibility you have to alter or modify your educational program. If something is not working, you can try something else. Support groups are a good source for helpful teaching tips and ideas.

Children need to understand a math concept before they can retain it.

What if my child has learning disabilities?

Most children occasionally have some trouble learning a new skill or understanding a new idea. This is normal—it is not a cause for concern. Persistent difficulties, however, require serious examination by a professional.

LEARNING DISABILITIES ARE COMMON

Every child occasionally has difficulty learning. This is perfectly normal; however, an increasing number of children are being diagnosed or referred to as learning disabled. Despite professional disagreement, the consensus is that as many as ten percent (up from five percent a few years ago) of children have some type of learning disability (Coles, Gerad. *The Learning Mystique*. Pantheon Books, 1987, pp. 9-10). The term "learning disability" is used as an umbrella to cover a variety of different labels such as minimal brain disorder (MBD), developmental aphasia, dyslexia, and attention deficit disorder (ADD)—sometimes accompanied with hyperactivity (ADHD). Although the specific label might vary, a common theme linking these disabilities is a problem with understanding or using language, spoken or written.

Many learning disabled children are smart children struggling to learn.

Children considered to have learning disabilities can struggle with a variety of skills: thinking, listening, speaking, reading, writing, spelling, or math.

These are skills students need to do their school work. Interestingly, lack of intelligence does not seem to be linked with learning disabilities. In fact, just the opposite is the case. Most "learning disabled" children are classified as average, if not above average, in intelligence (Healy, Jane M. *Endangered Minds*. Simon and Schuster, 1990, p. 141). Many learning disabled children are smart children struggling to learn which is all the more frustrating.

TYPES OF DISABILITIES

Dyslexia: Definitions of dyslexia vary, however, most dyslexics have trouble with reading and spelling. The problems usually become apparent in the early years of school when formal instruction begins. Some of the more commonly observed behaviors include reversing letters (b for d, p for q), reversing words (*was* for *saw*, *dog* for *god*), and seeing letters or words upside down. Reversals of letters and words can simply be developmental and are typical of emerging and beginning readers. However, if your child continues to struggle with visual perception of printed materials over a long period of time despite any instructional adjustments you might make, it may indicate a more serious problem.

If you suspect your child has dyslexia, seek professional help. Children identified by a professional as dyslexic can struggle with reading and reading-related subjects for most of their school career. A professional can be of great assistance in identifying specific teaching strategies that will work to help meet your child's specialized needs.

Attention Deficit Disorder (ADD): Another learning disability which has been on the rise in the last couple of decades is ADD (attention deficit disorder) or ADHD (attention deficit hyperactivity disorder). This rapid increase may be due to the fact that more children are being tested and diagnosed. As a general rule, ADD and ADHD children demonstrate difficulty concentrating and maintaining attention. If the task or skill is hard, uninteresting to the child, or irrelevant for the child; these difficulties are more pronounced. The most common complaints from teachers and parents about ADD and ADHD children is that these children are impetuous, disorganized, excitable, careless,

unpredictable, and prone to daydreaming. Ronald is an example of a child with attention deficit disorder accompanied by hyperactivity. He spends a great deal of his day darting about the house. His schoolwork is in every room. He can never find an assignment for his mom. He never stops moving and anything distracts him. When he was in the local school, he would crawl under his desk, stand on a table, and once even left his classroom by climbing out the second-story window and shinning down a tree. He was nine years old at the time and old enough to know better, but extremely impulsive. If you suspect an attention deficit disorder, seek professional advice.

As with dyslexia, the causes and diagnosis of ADD and ADHD are not always clear. A particular behavior may be characteristic of normal development or symptomatic of a learning disability. For example, a five-year-old will have difficulty attending to a task for an hour because five-year-olds usually have attention spans that range from ten to fifteen minutes.

Situational Learning Disabilities: A situational learning disability is one that appears only during certain types of activities, but may not be a disability at all. Situational learning disabilities often

Kids need to succeed and to believe they can succeed despite any difficulties they might need to overcome.

—Susan Hayes, 4 years home-school parent

occur during traditional types of schoolwork. For example, Donald is a nine-year-old boy who has been diagnosed with ADD. Donald has a hard time paying attention, especially when the schoolwork involves traditional paper-and-pencil tasks or extensive listening. It is a struggle for him to complete routine homework assignments. Because Donald doesn't keep his attention focused on the work, it often takes him hours to finish what should be a twenty-minute assignment. All the while, Donald's parents are coaxing and reminding him to finish the homework. Interestingly, this same boy can spend uninterrupted hours engrossed in comic books, Lego® blocks, or computer games. Since Donald *can* spend hours on these tasks, he does not have an attention deficit. If Donald's parents vary, modify, or substitute the educational task, the behaviors of concern are no longer evident. It's not that these situational "learning disabled" children can't learn, it's that they may have difficulty learning with certain approaches. Find the instructional approach that works best with your child.

It can be difficult as a parent to distinguish between a situational disability and manipulative behavior on the part of your child. It is wise to consult with family members as well as to ask opinions of educators concerning your child. These "outside" opinions may help us gain perspective on challenges we may encounter.

CAUSES OF DISABILITIES

There is no universal agreement as to the cause or causes of any particular learning disability. Many professionals believe that learning disabilities are over-diagnosed. This means that children are identified dyslexic or ADD when, in fact, they are not. Some professionals even question the existence of learning disabilities. Others object to the term being used in the sense that it implies some malfunction *within the child.*

Proposed causes for learning disabilities range from an inner ear problem to a low threshold for boredom. A more comprehensive list of possible explanations include:

- Prenatal exposure to alcohol, drugs, or other toxins.

- Underdevelopment of brain areas thought to be associated with learning in general and reading in particular.

- Insufficient quantities of neurotransmitters, the chemicals that help electro-chemical messages pass from brain cell to brain cell.

- The inability of the brain to distinguish the "fast" phonetic sounds in words.

- An unstable or stressful home environment.

- Frustration due to inappropriate classroom structure.

- Pressure due to required educational tasks for which the child is not yet equipped.

- Anxiety due to teaching techniques and procedures which do not meet needs or match learning style.

SEEK HELP

Home educating a child with learning disabilities is demanding in terms of time, energy, and emotions. You might find that your child's disability and related behaviors are persistent and encompassing to the point of complete frustration. If this happens, and you are not comfortable backing off or taking a wait-and-see approach, get an outside opinion. Contact a child psychologist, pediatrician, pediatric neurologist, special education teacher, educational therapist, or reading specialist. These professionals can offer new and useful perspectives and assistance. They might also help you to decide whether or not the home-education experience can be restructured in such a way that you and your child will experience success. Just remember that even "experts" can be wrong and do not agree on the causes, treatments, or even the existence of learning disabilities. A wise and reasonable approach would be to get professional input, carefully consider it, and make a decision based upon this input and what you know about your child.

Home educating a child with learning disabilities is demanding in terms of time, energy, and emotions.

The Cahill Family

Tim, Tammy

Tim (16)

Taylore (13)

Tawny (10)

Tysen (4)

Tori (1)

—5 Years

Home Schooling

Home schooling has been a wonderful way to have my children bond with their siblings. Unlike children who go in their own direction every morning, we share the same basic agenda. I feel this has made a substantial difference in the way my children have learned to care for one another. Large quantities of time have provided more opportunity for quality time.

One stormy day I stood back and watched my sixth-grade daughter teach her one-year-old brother about raindrops as she held him on her lap and they peered out the window. It is times like this that I feel privileged we are a home-school family. —Tammy Cahill, 5 years home-school mom

Finding the Balance

- How do I balance the demands of home schooling with the rest of my life?

- How do I avoid burnout?

- How do I integrate my values and beliefs?

How do I balance the demands of home schooling with the rest of my life?

Practical tips for organizing, planning ahead, and enlisting help will lighten the load for home-schooling parents.

I frequently use a crock pot to prepare dinner. When we arrive home from afternoon activities like sports, our food is ready and we sit down and enjoy dinner as a family.
—Juanita Lee, 4 years home-school parent

Somewhere near the end of the third month of home teaching, the initial euphoria of excitement and accomplishment often becomes clouded by feelings of panic as parents lament— *Help . . . How do I teach my kids and still accomplish everything else I've always done?* We are happy to report that there is a simple answer to this question: You don't—at least not at first.

The parent who is doing the primary teaching should view his or her role as a second job. No sensible person would attempt to work outside the home for four to five hours a day while still maintaining the exact schedule kept prior to working. The same is true when you assume the responsibility to home teach. Your schedule and time are greatly affected; some adjustments will need to be made. The following guidelines may prove helpful to you as you attempt to balance the demands of your increasingly busy schedule.

ORGANIZE YOUR LIVING SPACE

Since home schooling takes place in the home, specifically *your* home, it becomes increasingly important that it run smoothly and efficiently. Don't panic— there are many interpretations of what constitutes an efficiently-run household. One mother of four recently reported that on occasion, she considers the day a success if she can still find the phone to order out for pizza by the time her husband comes home in the evening!

Many of the most organized, successful parents we have worked with have adopted the philosophy that "less is better." They have decided to unclutter and organize their living and working space. One mother stated—*I found that the more possessions I owned, the busier I was caring for them and the less time I had for other more rewarding activities. I finally realized that I needed to give away a lot of things that were consistently getting in our way and find a place for the things we needed and enjoyed.*

If uncluttering and organizing your home sounds like an overwhelming task to you, start with small steps. Each week choose one area such as a closet, desk, or cabinet to unclutter. As you examine its contents ask yourself—*Do we need and/or really enjoy this item? Is it currently being used?* If the answer to these questions is "no," plan on getting rid of it. If the answer is "yes," find a place to store it near where it is used and make a commitment to return it there after each use. Efficiency is especially important now that there are more people in your home all day long and because home schooling requires new "stuff" to store and organize. If you haven't already dealt with the old "stuff," you too might find yourself searching for the phone at the end of a long day.

Once you have your living space organized, it's time to consider how you are going to organize your home-school materials. Though home schooling occurs in every room in the house and in the backyard and front yard as well, it is helpful to plan space for your home-school materials. Ask yourself these questions—*Where will we store and keep materials accessible for science and art? Where will we centralize or will we centralize our family library? Where will paper and record keeping supplies be kept?*

Will areas be designated where supplies can be left out or will supplies be put away each day? What will the guidelines be for each area so that learning can be maximized? When you plan answers to questions like these, it helps prevent misunderstandings. For example, the Jacksons did not set standards for their art area in their garage. The youngest member of the family did not know the pottery wheel and surrounding materials were off limits. The youngest ended up reshaping her older brother's ceramic "masterpiece" into an unidentifiable creation. Upon the discovery of the new "masterpiece," standards for the pottery area were immediately set. Situations like this can be disappointing—especially for older children—and are sometimes unavoidable—especially for younger children. Planning ahead, organizing materials, and setting standards help minimize confusion.

Many of the most organized, successful parents we have worked with have adopted the philosophy that "less is better."

CREATE A PLANNING NOTEBOOK

Planning takes time, but in the long run it saves you time and yields better results. The best tool we can recommend for home management is a planning notebook. This notebook will allow you to record your appointments, household chores, goals, and ideas all in one place. It will serve as a visual image of your time.

There are many excellent daily planners available for purchase. Be sure to look for one that provides ample space to list household chores and school-related responsibilities as well as appointments and phone calls. You might prefer to compile your own notebook by making copies of the Weekly Planning Sheet on page 169. These sheets can be compiled in a

notebook. You might want to add divider sections for lists of goals, shopping lists, menu plans, etc. Blank forms for several types of organizational helps can be found on pages 156–173.

> *I stay organized by using a monthly planner notebook. I take it wherever I go and record all of our activities and appointments. This helps me to manage my time better and to plan ahead.*
>
> *—Juanita Lee, 4 years home-school parent*

WEEKLY PLANNING SHEET

Day of the week	TO DO	TO CALL	APPOINTMENTS
SUNDAY	Check with Pat about filling in for Sunday School	Aunt June – "Happy Birthday"	Church 9-12
MONDAY	Mop kitchen floor 2 loads wash Finalize unit of study (China)	Plummer (kitchen drain) 766-8000 Julie Davis (unit ideas) 463-8911	4:00 p.m. Soccer
TUESDAY	Prepare for Co-op Teaching group	Kim (co-op Teaching jobs) 833-8888	1:00-2:30 Library w/kids 4:00 p.m. eye appt.
WEDNESDAY	Laundry - 2 loads		7:00 p.m. Pioneer girls
THURSDAY	Errands: Find materials for sculpting project. Dry cleaners Pick up photos	Cheryl (535-8161) Jenni (880-9966)	3:00 p.m. Ballet (Julie, Jenny)
FRIDAY	Complete next week's lesson plans Correct all outstanding assignments Weed back flower beds.		9:00-11:00 am Co-op Teaching group
SATURDAY	Menu planning Grocery shop Fertilize roses		8:00-10:00 am Soccer game 6:00 p.m. Dinner with Jeffersons

The first section of your notebook should contain a yearly calendar with a page for each month. This is your personal planning calendar that will help you remember commitments and respond to requests on time. Keep your calendar near the phone and check it daily. Write down meetings and engagements as you hear about them. Use your calendar to jog your memory for details to do, such as bringing art supplies to your support group meeting or returning library books. If you consistently record pertinent information on your calendar, you can throw away all the little reminder notes that have a way of accumulating around the house. A blank calendar for a month can be found on page 171.

Used effectively, your planning notebook will save you countless hours of frustration. It will allow you to coordinate the details between your teaching responsibilities and the other areas of your life.

You can relax (well, almost relax) knowing that all pertinent information is safe, sound, and located in one place!

POST A FAMILY CALENDAR

Buy and display a large family calendar and post it where it is accessible to all family members. Teach your older children to regularly check the calendar (you may want to make this part of your breakfast routine) and to record all upcoming dates and activities.

Coordinating family activities in this manner will save lots of tears, anxiety, and "high speed" dashes to the soccer field.

Coordinating family activities will save lots of tears, anxiety, and "high speed" dashes to the soccer field.

MAY 1995 calendar:

SUNDAY	MONDAY	TUESDAY	WEDNESDAY	THURSDAY	FRIDAY	SATURDAY
	1 5:00 Little League	2	3 7:00 Musical	4 10:00 Library	5 Home School	6 Conference
7 9-12 Church	8 5:00 Little League	9 7:00-9:00 Support Group	10 Natural History Museum	11	12	13 10:00 Story Hour at Library
14 9-12 Church	15 3:00 Dave's Dental appt. 5:00 Little League	16	17 Space Museum	18 10:00 Library	19 Janey spending night at Sarah's house	20
21 9-12 Church	22 5:00 Little League	23 7:00-9:00 Support Group	24 Vacation - Lake Arrowhead	25	26	27 10:00 Story Hour at Library
28 9-12 Church	29 5:00 Little League	30	31 Arboretum			

BE FLEXIBLE

Even with the best organizational plan, schedules, and notebook, there are simply going to be times when you need a break or a change of schedule to help you get your school and home chores completed. Tammy Cahill, who has five children and has home schooled five years, uses this morning plan—*I have the children start the day by working in independent study books. This gives me time in the morning to bathe the baby and tend to household chores. When I am finished, I am free to work with my school-age children.*

ENLIST OUTSIDE HELP

One thing home-schooling parents learn quickly is that there are not enough hours in the day to do everything! The parent who moves from full-time homemaker to homemaker/teacher often finds it difficult to ask for help and/or to get it if he or she does ask.

If your budget allows, hired help in any form is always a welcome relief. Many parents find that while they may not be able to afford a professional housekeeper on a regular basis, they can afford to hire help on an occasional basis, such as help with windows or major spring cleaning.

One idea that has worked for many families is to hire a high school student several hours a week to help with laundry, light cleaning, yard work, or baby-sitting. Hiring a dependable student can have many advantages:

1) Students are usually eager to learn and will complete the job according to *your* specifications.

2) Students are pleased to earn additional money and charge much less than a professional.

3) Your children will benefit from a positive role model.

INVOLVE YOUR CHILDREN IN HOUSEHOLD CHORES

Even if you can afford outside help to assist with household chores, you will need additional help from your children. Every member of your household should carry part of the load. The majority of children do not naturally observe when something needs to be done and rush quickly to do it. Rather, they need an organized system of instruction, incentive, and accountability. Initially this takes time on the part of the parent but it yields wonderful results, not only for you, but for your child.

There are many advantages to teaching your child to work at home:

1) Children learn responsibility.

2) Part of the work load is lifted from the home-school parent.

3) There is more time for fun activities with the children and more time for the parents to think, plan, and relax.

4) It helps alleviate symptoms of the "Mom is our maid" or "Dad is our servant" syndrome.

Working at home also fosters and stimulates the maturity process. Ready or not, your children are someday going to cook, clean, and care for themselves and, most likely, others. Teaching children to accomplish these tasks efficiently will be a tremendous advantage and will assist them in assuming responsibility and independence. Working at home also helps children feel needed as they realize they provide an intricate part in the smooth running of their household.

Working at home helps children feel needed as they realize they provide an intricate part in the smooth running of their household.

Hopefully, by now, you're convinced that it's in everyone's best interest for your children to assist in the household responsibilities. Here are a few tips to help make it happen:

1. Write down chore assignments. See example. You may wish to use the blank Household Chore Chart on page 170.

2. Set aside a regular time every day to accomplish chores.

3. Teach your child how to complete each job—don't assume your child knows how to do something just because he or she has seen you do it. Work with your child until he or she can complete a job independently.

4. Offer incentives—few children are mature enough to work from intrinsic motivation. Most children initially need extrinsic motivation when working toward new skills and habits. This can be as simple as a star on a chore chart or an elaborate system of earned privileges. Take time to find what works for your child.

5. Be consistent. You will need to provide consistent follow-up. The greatest system ever designed is futile if it isn't consistently executed.

ENLIST HELP IN SCHOOL-RELATED RESPONSIBILITIES

Knowing that you are totally responsible for your child's education can be, at times, overwhelming. Some families are blessed with extended family members who want to participate in this learning adventure. One lucky fifth-grade boy receives his science instruction from his grandmother, his foreign language instruction from his grandfather, and his reading/literature instruction from his father. His mother teaches the remaining subjects and coordinates schedules and assignments to provide continuity for his entire program.

Some parents join with other parents to hire tutors for small-group instruction for specific subjects such as math or science. Still others participate in a co-op teaching plan in which parents rotate teaching subjects.

If you are currently doing *everything* and feel the need to ease up on some of your responsibilities, seriously consider enlisting help.

BE KIND TO YOURSELF

A key principle that will serve you in finding and keeping your balance is to treat yourself with the same love and respect that you provide for your family.

When life feels overwhelming, stand back, review your initial reasons for home schooling, attempt to reclaim the "big picture," and then indulge in a favorite activity just for you. Perhaps it's spending some extra time with a wonderful book or maybe it's an afternoon at the mall or a local arboretum. It's easy to fall into the "I don't have time for myself" trap. We all need time to refurbish our minds, bodies, and spirits. Your children benefit from seeing their parents actively engaged in activities that are interesting and enjoyable. When you take time for yourself, not only you, but your whole family benefits.

Last, but not least, keep in mind that home schooling is one of the most challenging tasks a family can endeavor. It takes teamwork to make it a successful experience for all. The wise home-school family gathers as many team members as possible—spouse, children, extended family, and friends.

The wise home-school family gathers as many team members as possible—spouse, children, extended family, and friends.

How do I avoid burnout?

Being a parent can be a challenging and exhausting job. Being parent *and* teacher intensifies this experience.

Stress is a given. A new baby, twin toddlers, an ailing grandparent, a house under construction, part-time or nighttime employment, volunteer responsibilities, —all these added to the role of parent and teacher create a challenging experience.

KNOW YOUR CHILD'S LEARNING STYLE

Learning is always more difficult for a child when there is a mismatch between teaching strategy and the child's learning style. Using flash cards with an auditory learner is an example of a learning style mismatch. Other examples of mismatch include: relying too much on oral directions when teaching a visual learner, requiring too much paper-and-pencil activity for a kinesthetic learner, not allowing an extroverted student time for trial-and-error learning, and over-emphasizing facts and details with an intuitive learner (they value imagination and inspiration). Instructional mismatch can occur anywhere within the modality-temperament-intelligence type framework. Striving to establish a match between your teaching strategy and your child's individual learning style will result in a more pleasant instructional experience for both you and your child.

ALLOW MISTAKES

Some parents feel stress when their child makes mistakes however, mistakes can provide splendid opportunities for you to discover how your child thinks and learns. Several years ago, this author was administering a test to a child. One particular question designed to measure mental computation ability went something like this: You buy a twelve-pound

> *When we face burnout, we need to consider if we are demanding too much of our children.*
>
> *—Susan Hayes, 4 years home-school parent*

turkey that takes thirty minutes per pound to cook. At what time should you put the turkey in the oven in order for dinner to be ready at 5:00 p.m.? The boy being tested gave an "incorrect" answer. When questioned on how he arrived at his answer, he indicated that he had included additional time to set the table and to prepare the house for visitors. When he was asked to just focus on the turkey, he gave the "correct" response. Consider the thoughtfulness with which he attacked the problem. He turned a dry math problem into a real-life situation and as a result came up with the "wrong" answer—wrong, that is, to the authors of the test. His answer was right if the situation was real and relevant. His supposed error was a sign of more complex thought than was expected of him. Had he not had the opportunity to explain his mistake, he would have been penalized with a lower score for his ingenuity. Yes, there is a lesson here beyond the accuracy of test scores. The lesson is this: Do not accept answers at face value. Your child can actually have a very logical explanation for an answer, no matter how nonsensical or inaccurate that answer seems. It certainly does no harm to ask how your child arrived at his or her answer—you might uncover something about how your child thinks.

MEET NEEDS BY PLAYING GAMES

Children have at least four basic needs beyond food, love, and shelter. These four needs are belonging, power, freedom, and fun (Glasser, William. *Control Theory in the Classroom*. HarperCollins, 1986). If not met, children will expend their energies trying to satisfy these needs. The educational process will be disrupted, sometimes quite literally. Playing games provides an opportunity to meet these needs:

1. Games are often a social activity, providing interpersonal interaction and opportunities for interdependent actions. (belonging)

2. The concept of power and control is intrinsic in most games. The game player is generally submitting his or herself to control and command by others, assuming control and command of others, or competing for control and command with others. (power)

3. Games allow a child to deal with aggressive and competitive urges in socially acceptable ways. Games are an exercise in controlled and adaptive expressions of aggression. (freedom)

4. Almost by definition, games are enjoyable. (fun)

Recess is a must. A 15 to 20-minute break after one to two hours is essential. It will help both you and your children relax and refocus your energies.
—Shirley Ford, 3 years home-school parent

In addition to meeting basic needs, playing games can contribute to positive attitudes regarding self, specific skills and subjects, and learning in general. Games can provide a non-threatening atmosphere for instruction. In order to play a game, most children will readily and enthusiastically learn the same academic skills that they consider difficult or uninspiring when presented as "schoolwork."

Games can provide a nonthreatening atmosphere for instruction.

Games can be a relatively painless way to review skills or facts. Sometimes this feature is built into the game (e.g., Scrabble®). Commercial games can be modified to review or practice skills. If you are energetic, enjoy a challenge, and have the time, you can create games to meet the specific needs of your children.

The type of game that appeals to your child will be a factor of his or her learning style. Visual learners are comfortable with board games, whereas kinesthetic learners usually prefer games involving skill, balance, action, and physical competition. Auditory learners generally enjoy word games and games involving questions and answers. Word games also appeal to children of linguistic intelligence. Strategy and math games appeal to children of logical-mathematical intelligence. Children of visual-spatial intelligence enjoy puzzles, mazes, board and map games, and visual-spatial games such as Battleship®. Children of bodily-kinesthetic intelligence, similar to children of the kinesthetic modality, respond well to games involving action, skill, excitement, and competition. Group games and cooperative games appeal to children of interpersonal intelligence. Solo games attract children of intrapersonal intelligence. Of course, game preference based on learning style describes general inclinations, not fixed categories.

You do not have an obligation to keep your child constantly entertained. That is a skill that your child needs to develop. Game play is, however, an alternative instructional strategy that may be a solution for a child who resists or struggles with more traditional approaches. Games can facilitate emotional growth, self-expression, and self-esteem. Games can also contribute to the development of cognitive skills (concentration, memory, creative problem solving), academic skills, and social skills. In summary, playing games with your child can be more than just a diversion or break from routine home education. Games can become a valuable and effective instructional strategy for relieving instructional stress. See page 187 for a list of recommended games.

PLAN SPECIAL TIMES FOR THE FAMILY

Planning special times for the family, such as special days or family vacations, is a must. Jenni Key, a home-school mom with nine years of experience, has found that "first days" are a special way to celebrate the simple things in life—*Through the years, my kids have looked forward to "first" days: the first day of school that it rains, we have hot cocoa and do our schoolwork in front of the fire; the first day of a season (autumn, winter, spring, summer), we take a walk on the bridal trail and enjoy seasonal changes; the first day of a holiday season, we decorate the school-room—set up a small Christmas tree, hang valentines from the ceiling, fill grass baskets with eggs, etc.* These celebrations add a sense of fun and simplicity and provide needed breaks from the school routine. Special times need not be expensive. They can be very simple.

Games can become a valuable and effective instructional strategy for relieving instructional stress.

A complete change of pace also provides a fresh outlook. John Lee, home-school parent of five years, describes his family's unique experience—*Because my job requires frequent business travel, home schooling allows our children to occasionally travel with me while continuing their schooling. We can take advantage of museums, historical landmarks, and other experiences that traveling outside the local community offers.*

SET ASIDE TIME FOR YOURSELF

A teaching parent needs time to plan, record learning activities, and gather teaching materials on a regular basis. This time needs to be time *away* from the kids—perhaps during nap time, early in the morning, or late in the evening after the kids have gone to bed. You also might think about teaming with another home-school parent, other adult members of your household, neighbors, or friends to coordinate a regular planning/record-keeping time. For most home-school parents, time alone is essential for maintaining sanity.

KEEP PLANS FLEXIBLE AND FLUID

Flexibility and informality can often ease the stress that a home-school parent feels. Joyce Ulshafer, who has seven years of home-schooling experience, saves frustration in her planning by doing the following—*I tend to be informal in teaching my K–3 children. Instead of making out detailed plans, I have "skeleton lesson plans." I add details to the plans after the fact. It saves a lot of erasing and frustration. My lessons are more like a diary.* This practical diary approach has saved time and frustration for many experienced home-school parents. It also gives parents the opportunity to keep their plans flexible and fluid to meet the need of the moment.

Joyce Ulshafer keeps flexibility in her plans by accommodating her children's needs to move about. She writes—*For my "non-workbook" children, doing practice math problems on our white board or even out on the driveway with colored chalk is a nice change of pace.* As the old adage goes—"Variety is the spice of life." Be flexible. Change plans. Accommodate needs at the moment. Remember it's okay if you don't follow your lesson plans exactly. Think of your plans as a *general* guide and the rest will fall into place.

> *A teaching parent needs time to plan, record learning activities, and gather teaching materials on a regular basis.*

KEEP A SENSE OF HUMOR

Sometimes we become so obsessed with the need to do everything perfect that we forget to have fun, laugh, and enjoy life. Keep a sense of humor.

Team teaching or shared units provides a "shot-in-the-arm" for people approaching burnout.

—Susan Hayes, 4 years home-school parent

How do I integrate my values and beliefs?

Integrating values and beliefs in the home-school setting can be realized through communication, modeling, and monitoring curriculum and extracurricular activities.

COMMUNICATION

Day-by-day issues are opportunities for you to communicate your values with your child. If, for instance, you are using curriculum materials and you come across a unit or section that is contrary to your values and beliefs, try to turn it into a positive experience. For example, one parent used a unit on mythology as an opportunity to do a comparative study between the character of the gods men create and the character of God in the *Bible*. This study helped the child to become familiar with mythology as well as to clarify and synthesize some of his or her personal beliefs.

Another opportunity for integrating values and beliefs in your home is during the daily conversations that you have with your child. One adult said in looking back on her childhood—*I could talk to my parents about anything—drugs, pregnancy, what my peers were doing—without being questioned as to why I wanted to talk about it. They were always open and ready to talk.* By listening to your children, you gain insight into their thinking. Open communication gives your children a "safety net" in which to explore and clarify their values.

MODELING

Your day-to-day living models the values and beliefs by which you govern your life. Whether or not you are aware of it, your children constantly absorb and learn your values. As the old proverb says, "Actions speak louder than words." If you teach patience but constantly lose it, your child will learn the latter. Of course, you, the role model, are not perfect. You will fail from time to time. Then your child will have the opportunity to see you model the importance of being honest and learning from life's mistakes. Day in and day out, your life models your values and beliefs and touches and molds the life of your child. It's a tremendous responsibility with tremendous rewards.

CURRICULUM

As a home-schooling parent, you can choose a curriculum that supports your values, beliefs, and academic goals. Each year more and more curriculum is developed specifically for home-school students. Many language arts programs use the classics to teach character development and values. Many parents find it is unnecessary to purchase a special "values" curriculum. Rather, they have found that any story can be a springboard for discussion as they compare and contrast the values represented in the story with the values their family holds.

Some parents choose religious curriculum materials, along with their academic curriculum materials, to support the teaching that their children already receive from their church, temple, or synagogue. Many families find daily, systematic study of their religious beliefs helpful in giving their children a solid foundation in their religion. Access to religious curriculum is most easily available through your religious organization.

EXTRACURRICULAR ACTIVITIES

Monitoring extracurricular activities is one way parents integrate their values and beliefs. For example, if you believe the media can be violent and extreme, then you can carefully monitor the movies your child sees. You are in a great position to assess what's appropriate and what will have a positive impact on your child. You also are in a position to influence who the people are with whom your child spends most of his or her free time.

Extracurricular activities can also include activities that support your curriculum (e.g., field trips, sports teams, music lessons). Together, you and your child can plan enrichment classes which are supportive, or at least not contradictory to, your family's basic values and beliefs.

Home schooling takes some investment and changes in lifestyle, but the rewards are overwhelming.
—Gwen Fisher, 2 years home-school parent

FAMILY RELATIONSHIPS

Home school is also a prime opportunity to strengthen the bonds between you and your children and between the children themselves. Juanita Lee, home-school parent of four years writes—

When our firstborn became a brother for the first time, we told him that he and the new baby were selected to be lifelong friends. We emphasized friendship-building skills in our sons' relationships to one another. Our goals are that they will remain close friends throughout their lives and that these skills will help to build strong relationships with others outside our family. Love, support, and friendship between family members are character qualities that will strengthen the family. This solid base of supportive relationships can provide an example for your child to follow in relationships outside the home as well as provide emotional support for your child throughout his or her lifetime.

Overwhelmingly, home-schooling parents agree that the increased impact they have on their children's lives is worth the time, money, and commitment they are investing. Tassie Hare, who has eight years of home-schooling experience, puts it all in perspective—*I am raising citizens for tomorrow's society. If I can remember that teaching my children manners, values, persistence, and perseverance is just as important as math, English, handwriting, and science—then I've gone a long way in raising successful children who will excel in whatever areas they decide to pursue.*

Home educating your children is indeed a unique privilege—one that allows you not only to impart academic knowledge but wisdom and values. Day by day as you teach math, English, and geography, you also shape attitudes, reinforce beliefs, and provide a safe haven in which your children can grow, question, and explore. We strongly believe that your investment in this educational process will provide lifelong dividends for you and your children which will strengthen the family as well as the community at large. Our best wishes to you and your family in all your educational endeavors.

> *Home educating your children is indeed a unique privilege—one that allows you not only to impart academic knowledge but wisdom and values.*

Resources

- Reproducibles

- Curriculum Resources

- Government Agencies

- Support Groups

- Testing Materials

- Commercial Learning Games

- Bibliography

- Glossary

ATTENDANCE CALENDAR

NAME: _____ / _____ / _____
LAST   FIRST   M.I.

TEACHER: _____

ADDRESS: _____
STREET

_____ / _____
STATE   ZIP

GRADE: _____ SCHOOL YEAR: _____

BIRTH DATE: _____ / _____ / _____
YEAR   MONTH   DATE

TOTAL DAYS OF ATTENDANCE: _____

KEY: E = ENROLLED   / = DAY OF INSTRUCTION   S = SICK (OPTIONAL)   H = HOLIDAY (OPTIONAL)   BLANK = NO SCHOOL

DATE	AUG.	SEPT.	OCT.	NOV.	DEC.	JAN.	FEB.	MAR.	APR.	MAY	JUNE	JULY
1												
2												
3												
4												
5												
6												
7												
8												
9												
10												
11												
12												
13												
14												
15												
16												
17												
18												
19												
20												
21												
22												
23												
24												
25												
26												
27												
28												
29												
30												
31												
TOTALS												

TOTAL DAYS OF INSTRUCTION _____

COURSE OF STUDY

NAME: _____ SCHOOL: _____

SCHOOL YEAR: _____ GRADE: _____ AGE: _____

SUBJECT	TEXTS	ADDITIONAL MATERIALS

Home Schooling ©1995 Creative Teaching Press, Inc.

EVALUATION

NAME: _____ **SCHOOL YEAR:** _____ **GRADE:** _____

SEMESTER 1	SEMESTER 2

Evaluation

MY CHILD'S STRENGTHS AND WEAKNESSES

NAME: _____ AGE: _____ GRADE LEVEL: _____

In the chart below, describe your child's strengths and weaknesses.

STRENGTHS	WEAKNESSES
Reading	
Math	
Language Arts	
Science	
Social Studies	
Emotional	
Spiritual	
Social	
Physical	

LONG-TERM PLANNING

Textbook-Driven

List concepts/topics you will cover each month. You may wish to specify chapter units or page numbers.

AUGUST

Reading:

Language Arts:

Math:

Social Studies:

Science:

SEPTEMBER

Reading:

Language Arts:

Math:

Social Studies:

Science:

OCTOBER

Reading:

Language Arts:

Math:

Social Studies:

Science:

NOVEMBER

Reading:

Language Arts:

Math:

Social Studies:

Science:

DECEMBER

Reading:

Language Arts:

Math:

Social Studies:

Science:

JANUARY

Reading:

Language Arts:

Math:

Social Studies:

Science:

LONG-TERM PLANNING

Textbook-Driven

List concepts/topics you will cover each month. You may wish to specify chapter units or page numbers.

FEBRUARY	MARCH
Reading:	Reading:
Language Arts:	Language Arts:
Math:	Math:
Social Studies:	Social Studies:
Science:	Science:

APRIL	MAY
Reading:	Reading:
Language Arts:	Language Arts:
Math:	Math:
Social Studies:	Social Studies:
Science:	Science:

JUNE	JULY
Reading:	Reading:
Language Arts:	Language Arts:
Math:	Math:
Social Studies:	Social Studies:
Science:	Science:

Long-Term Planning (Textbook Driven)

YEARLY PLANNING SHEET
Theme-Driven

AUGUST

Unit Concept:

Math Concepts:

Other:

SEPTEMBER

Unit Concept:

Math Concepts:

Other:

OCTOBER

Unit Concept:

Math Concepts:

Other:

NOVEMBER

Unit Concept:

Math Concepts:

Other:

DECEMBER

Unit Concept:

Math Concepts:

Other:

JANUARY

Unit Concept:

Math Concepts:

Other:

Home Schooling ©1995 Creative Teaching Press, Inc.

Long-Term Planning (Theme-Driven)

YEARLY PLANNING SHEET

Theme-Driven

FEBRUARY

Unit Concept:

Math Concepts:

Other:

MARCH

Unit Concept:

Math Concepts:

Other:

APRIL

Unit Concept:

Math Concepts:

Other:

MAY

Unit Concept:

Math Concepts:

Other:

JUNE

Unit Concept:

Math Concepts:

Other:

JULY

Unit Concept:

Math Concepts:

Other:

Long-Term Planning (Theme-Driven)

UNIT PLANNING SHEET

UNIT: _____ DATES: _____

Reading Materials

Independent:

Read Alouds:

Language Arts / Writing Activities:

Social Studies:

Science:

Art:

Math:

Music:

Cooking:

Physical Education:

Supplies Needed:

Related Field Trips:

Home Schooling ©1995 Creative Teaching Press, Inc.

WEEKLY ASSIGNMENT SHEET

NAME: _____ GRADE: _____ WEEK OF: _____

SUBJECT	MONDAY	TUESDAY	WEDNESDAY	THURSDAY	FRIDAY
Reading					
Language Arts					
Math					
Social Studies					
Science					
Art, Music, P.E., Health, Other					

Weekly Assignment Sheet

LEARNING LOG

NAME: _____   GRADE: _____   WEEK OF: _____

SUBJECT	MONDAY	TUESDAY	WEDNESDAY	THURSDAY	FRIDAY
Reading					
Language Arts					
Math					
Social Studies					
Science					
Art, Music, P.E., Health, Other					

Home Schooling ©1995 Creative Teaching Press, Inc.

DAILY SCHEDULE
COORDINATING SEVERAL CHILDREN

⏰	CHILD ONE _____	CHILD TWO _____	CHILD THREE _____
7:00-8:00 a.m.			
8:00-9:00 a.m.			
9:00-10:00 a.m.			
10:00-11:00 a.m.			
LUNCH			
1:00-2:00 p.m.			
2:00-3:00 p.m.			

ORAL READING STANDARDS

	YES	NO	BETTER
1. I spoke up loudly enough for all to hear.			
2. I pronounced my words clearly.			
3. I held by head so that the audience could see my face.			
4. I looked at the audience as often as I could without losing my place.			
5. I read in word groups instead of word by word.			
6. When reading informational material, I read it slowly and clearly the way the author would talk.			
7. When reading conversations, I read the lines as the characters would have said them.			

My goal for next time:

_____

_____

_____

_____

EDITORIAL INSPECTION STANDARDS

The last steps in successful writing are editing and proofreading.

Use the editorial tips listed below to help you decide if your work is complete.

Structure	YES	NO
1. Is the main idea clearly stated in the topic sentence?		
2. Do the sentences that follow the topic sentence give supporting details?		
3. Does each new paragraph begin a new idea?		
4. Do all the sentences express a complete thought?		
Mechanics		
5. Is the first word of each paragraph indented?		
6. Does each sentence and each proper noun begin with a capital letter?		
7. Does each sentence have the correct punctuation mark?		
8. Did I check spelling?		

My goal for next time:

_____

_____

_____

_____

Home Schooling ©1995 Creative Teaching Press, Inc.

WEEKLY PLANNING SHEET

Day of the week	TO DO	TO CALL	APPOINTMENTS
SUNDAY			
MONDAY			
TUESDAY			
WEDNESDAY			
THURSDAY			
FRIDAY			
SATURDAY			

WEEK OF: _____

HOUSEHOLD CHORE CHART

WEEK OF: _____

CHORE	PERSON RESPONSIBLE					

Home Schooling ©1995 Creative Teaching Press, Inc.

Household Chore Chart

MONTH: _____

YEAR: _____

SUNDAY	MONDAY	TUESDAY	WEDNESDAY	THURSDAY	FRIDAY	SATURDAY

Monthly Calendar

Home Schooling ©1995 Creative Teaching Press, Inc.

LESSON PLANS FOR TWO CHILDREN

DATES: _____ STUDENTS: _____ / _____

TOGETHER:	
Monday	
Tuesday	
Wednesday	
Thursday	
Friday	

	Name: _____ Grade: _____	Name: _____ Grade: _____
Monday Math: Indep. Reading: Other:		
Tuesday Math: Indep. Reading: Other:		
Wednesday Math: Indep. Reading: Other:		
Thursday Math: Indep. Reading: Other:		
Friday Math: Indep. Reading: Other:		

DAILY GOAL SHEET

NAME: _____ DATE: _____

MORNING			
ORDER IN WHICH I WILL WORK	**WORK TO DO**	**TIME STARTED**	**TIME COMPLETED**
AFTERNOON			
EVALUATION		**YES**	**NO**
	My work was finished on time?		
	My work was done carefully?		

Curriculum Resources

This list of curriculum resources will help you get started in locating quality materials for your children. Home schoolers in your area may have additional curriculum resource recommendations. (Addresses and telephone numbers were current at time of printing.)

A Beka Book Publications
P.O. Box 18000
Pensacola, FL 32523-9160
(800) 874-2352
(800) 874-3590 FAX

Christian textbooks and supplies for PreK–12. Comprehensive video and correspondence programs available—includes all subjects for every grade level. Includes record keeping and earned diplomas. Free catalog.

Abbott Integration
Unit 110, 12871 Clarke Place
Richmond, British Columbia V6V 2H9
(604) 244-8798
(604) 244-8799 FAX

Computer hardware, software, and accessories.

A.D.S. Academic Distribution Services
528 Carnarvon St.
New Westminster, British Columbia V3L 1C4
(604) 524-9758
(800) 276-0078
(604) 540-8730 FAX

Supplier to home schoolers. Catalog describes a variety of text and workbook series: Alpha Omega, ACE, Usborne books, Bob Jones readers, Saxon Math, high school French, Canadian Social Studies, Learning Language through Literature, and Writing Strands. Catalog for minimal cost upon request. Canadian achievement testing also available.

Addison-Wesley Publishing Co., Inc.
1 Jacob Way
Reading, MA 01867
(800) 552-2259
(800) 333-3328 FAX

Textbooks for all subjects for grades kindergarten through college. Many home-school parents enjoy using the manipulative math series *Math Their Way*. Ask for specific information on setting up a home-school account.

AIMS Educational Foundation
1595 S. Chestnut Ave.
Fresno, CA 93702
(209) 255-4094
(209) 255-6396 FAX

Hands-on activities that combine math and science. Materials are available for grades K–9.

Alberta Education: Learning Resources Distributing Centre
12360 142nd St.
Edmonton, Alberta T5L 4X9
(403) 427-2767
(403) 422-9750 FAX

Extensive catalog of curriculum guides, textbooks, and other learning materials at all levels K–12. Mail order only. Charge for catalog.

Artel Educational Resources
5528 Kingsway
Burnaby, British Columbia V5H 2G2
(800) 665-9255 in Canada
(604) 435-4949 Vancouver
(604) 435-1955 FAX

Canadian representative for many publishers, including Educators Publishing Service. Supplier of a wide variety of consumable and reproducible workbooks in all subject areas. They also have high-interest/low-vocabulary materials appropriate for K–adult.

Arthur Bornstein School of Memory Training
11693 San Vicente Blvd.
Los Angeles, CA 90049
(800) 468-2058
(310) 207-2433 FAX

Home study memory courses for adults and children. Materials include techniques for learning foreign languages, study skills, multiplication tables, spelling, vocabulary, states, and capitals.

Artistoplay, Ltd.
P.O. Box 7529
Ann Arbor, MI 48107
(313) 995-4353
(800) 634-7738
(313) 995-4611 FAX

Unique literature, social studies, and science games. Most of the games are multilevel and can be played by the whole family. Free catalog.

Bob Jones University Press
Greenville, SC 29614
(800) 845-5731
(803) 242-5100, ext. 3300
(800) 525-8398

Christ-centered educational materials and science lab materials. Free catalog.

Bonjour Books
#2135-11871 Horseshoe Way
Richmond, British Columbia V7A 5H5
(604) 271-2665
(800) 665-8002
(604) 274-2665 FAX

Catalog of Eyewitness Books and a variety of French and English books.

Canadian Home Education Resources
7 Stanley Cr. S.W.
Calgary, Alberta T2S 1G1
(403) 243-9727
(800) 345-2952 for orders only

Free catalog of a wide variety of curriculum, texts, and games covering all subject areas.

Chinaberry Book Service
2780 Via Orange Way, Suite B
Spring Valley, CA 91978
(800) 776-2242
(619) 670-5203

Outstanding literature books and other treasures (craft kits, stickers, games, journals) for the entire family. Free catalog.

Christian Liberty Press
502 W. Euclid Avenue
Arlington Heights, IL 60004
(847) 259-4444
(847) 259-9972 FAX

Full service K–12 home school program. Achievement testing service and writing evaluation service. Publisher and distributor of Christ–centered materials. Free catalog.

Cobblestone Publishing
7 School St.
Peterborough, NH 03458
(603) 924-7209
(800) 821-0115
(603) 924-73880 FAX

Publishers of four quality children's magazines—*Cobblestone* (U.S. History), *Calliope* (World History), *Faces* (World Culture), *Odyssey* (science with focus on space and astronomy).

Creative Teaching Press, Inc.
P.O. Box 6017
Cypress, CA 90630-0017
(714) 995-7888
(800) 444-4287
(714) 995-3548 FAX

Educational books on a variety of subject areas, teaching aids, and supplies. Many theme-driven materials.

Critical Thinking Press and Software
P.O. Box 448
Pacific Grove, CA 93950
(800) 458-4849
(408) 393-3288
(408) 393-3277 FAX

Free catalog of thinking skills activity books and software.

Cuisenaire Company of America
10 Bank St.
White Plains, NY 10602-5026
(800) 237-3142
(800) 551-RODS

Free catalog of math manipulatives.

Curriculum Associates
5 Esquire Road
North Billerica, MA 01862-2589
(800) 225-0248
(508) 667-5706 FAX

Alternative materials for reading, spelling, math, and study skills. Free catalog.

Dale Seymour Publications
P.O. Box 10888
Palo Alto, CA 94303
(800) 872-1100
(415) 324-3424 FAX

Supplemental teaching materials for grades K–12: problem solving, thinking skills, language arts, math, and science. Free catalog.

D.C. Heath & Company
2700 N. Richardt Ave.
Indianapolis, IN 46219
(800) 428-8071
(800) 824-7390 FAX

Basic educational texts in all subject areas. Free catalog.

Delta Education
P.O. Box 950
Hudson, NH 03051
(800) 442-5444
(800) 282 9560

Free catalog of hands-on science resource materials.

EDC Publishing/Usborne Books
P.O. Box 470663
Tulsa, OK 74147-0663
(800) 475-4522
(800) 747-4509 FAX

A wide range of colorfully illustrated educational books for children of all ages. Science and history books are exceptional. Catalog for minimal cost. Rights to distribute Usborne books to U.S. See Riverwood Publishers for Canadian purchases.

Educational Alternatives, Inc., of Superior
1505 North 8th St.
Superior, WI 54880
(800) 219-2175
(715) 395-3482 FAX

Distributor of supplemental teaching materials in subject areas such as early learning, arts and crafts, music, games, computer software, language arts, math, science, social studies, and electronic education. Free catalog.

Edmund Scientific Company
101 East Gloucester Pike
Barrington, NJ 08007-1380
(609) 573-6260
(609) 573-6295 FAX

Science resource materials. Free catalog.

Exclusive Educational Products
243 Saunders Road
Barrie, Ontario L4M 6E7
(705) 725-1166
(800) 563-1166
(705) 725-1167 FAX

Free K–12 catalog of games, books, and manipulatives.

Family Pastimes
RR 4
Perth, Ontario K7H 3C6
(613) 267-4819
(613) 264-0696 FAX

Makers and distributors of 70 clever and enjoyable games for PreK–12. The basis for all these games is cooperation, not competition.

Glencoe/McGraw-Hill
P.O. 543
860 Taylor Station Road
Blacklick, OH 43004
(800) 334-7344
(614) 860-1877 FAX

Texts and teachers' manuals for all major subject areas for grades 6–12.

Globe Book Company, Simon & Schuster School Group
4350 Equity Dr.
Columbus, OH 43216
(800) 848-9500
(614) 771-7360 FAX

Excellent materials for creative writing and journalism. Free catalog.

Good Year Books
1900 East Lake Ave.
Glenview, IL 60025
(800) 628-4480, ext. 3038
(708) 729-8910 FAX

Resource materials for parents and teachers in all curricular areas, PreK–10. Free catalog.

Hammond, Inc.
515 Valley St.
Maplewood, NJ 07040
(800) 526-4953
(201) 763-7658 FAX

Geography materials, including maps and atlases. Free catalog.

Heathkit Educational Systems
455 Riverview Dr.
Benton Harbor, MI 49022
(800) 253-0570
(616) 925-4876

Secondary electronics courses in video, computer, and book format. Free catalog.

Hewitt Research Foundation
P.O. Box 9
Washougal, WA 98671
(800) 348-1750

Materials and books specifically for home schoolers. Free catalog and special needs packet. Counseling, texts, book lists and curriculum for all areas of special needs.

Houghton Mifflin/McDougal Littell Company
13400 Midway Road
Dallas, TX 75244
(800) 733-2828
(800) 733-2098

Textbooks and teachers' manuals for all subject areas for grades K–12. A letter of authorization from a school or an affidavit is required for ordering. Free catalog.

John Holt's Book & Music Store
2269 Massachusetts Ave.
Cambridge, MA 02140
(617) 864-3100
(617) 864-9235 FAX

Books and supplies with an interest-driven emphasis. Bimonthly magazine titled *Growing without Schooling*.

KONOS
P.O. Box 1534
Richardson, TX 75083-1534
(214) 669-8337
(214) 699-7922

Home-education curriculum materials with a Christian, theme-driven emphasis. Especially useful when home-educating more than one child. Free catalog.

Lakeshore Learning Materials
P.O. Box 6261
Carson, CA 90749
(800) 421-5354
(310) 537-5403

General educational supplies, games, and materials for PreK–3. For middle and high school students struggling with reading, request *Basics and Beyond* catalogue for high-interest/low-vocabulary materials. Free catalog.

Landmark Editions, Inc.
1402 Kansas Ave.
P.O. Box 4469
Kansas City, MO 64127
(816) 241-4919
(816) 483-3755 FAX

Offers a teacher's manual by David Melton titled *Written & Illustrated by. . .* to assist in helping students write and illustrate their own books. Also offers an annual contest titled *The National Written & Illustrated By. . .Awards Contest for Students.* The procedures for writing, illustrating, and making a book are designed for a group of children, but can be adapted for individual students. Winners of the annual writing contest get their books published. For a copy of the contest rules and guidelines, send an addressed, business-size envelope with $1.00 for postage and handling to the P.O. box above.

Lawrence Hall of Science
University of California
Berkeley, CA 94720
(510) 642-1016
(510) 642-1055 FAX

Free K–12 catalog of teachers' guides to assist in teaching math and science.

Master Desk Home School Supplies
P.O. Box 152
Sexsmith, Alberta T0H 3C0
(403) 568-2042

Quality curriculum, teaching aids, and resources for families—most written from a Christian perspective.

Mind Trek
2307 130th St.
White Rock, British Columbia V4A 8Y4
(604) 535-9180

Supplier of challenging and enriching games, tapes, and related materials. Free catalog.

Moore Canada Child Development Centre
4684 Darin Court
Kelowna, British Columbia V1W 2B3
(604) 764-4379

Materials written and researched by the home-school movement's founders. Send a self-addressed, stamped envelope for a select book list based on the low-stress Moore formula. Offers a variety of educational services, including legal defense.

Moore Foundation
Box #1
Camas, WA 98607
(360) 835-2736

Materials written and researched by the home-school movement's founders. Send a self-addressed, stamped envelope for a select book list based on the low-stress Moore formula. Offers a variety of educational services, including legal defense.

More Than Books. . .
146 McClintock Way
Kanata, Ontario K2L 2A4
(613) 592-5338

Free K–8 catalog of a wide range of supplies, curriculum materials, and books.

National Geographic Society
P.O. Box 2895
Washington, D.C. 20013
(202) 857-700
(800) 368-2728
(301) 921-1380 FAX

Geography magazines, supplies, and videos.

National Wildlife Federation

8925 Leesburg Pike
Vienna, VA 22184-0001
(800) 432-6564
(800) 822-9919
(703) 442-7332 FAX

Nature magazines for all ages, including *Your Big Backyard* for ages 3–5, *Ranger Rick* for ages 6–12, *National Wildlife* for ages 13–adult, *International Wildlife* for ages 13–adult. *Nature Scope* science workbook series also available on a variety of topics.

Rand McNally

P.O. Box 7600
Chicago, IL 60680
(800) 678-7263
(800) 934-3479

Atlases, maps, and children's travel books for ages 7–12. Free catalog.

Riverwood Publishers/Usborne Books

6 Dolands Ave.
P.O. Box 70
Sharon, Ontario L0G 1V0
(905) 478-8396
(800) 461-6858 FAX

A wide range of colorfully illustrated educational books for children of all ages. Science and history books are exceptional. Catalog for minimal cost. Rights to distribute Usborne books to Canada only. See EDC Publishing for U.S. purchases.

Saxon Publishers, Inc.

1320 West Lindsey, Suite 100
Norman, OK 73069
(405) 329-7071
(800) 284-7019
(405) 360-4205 FAX

Math, algebra, physics, and calculus texts; kits; and supplemental materials. All written with incremental development and an emphasis on drill and review. Catalog and K–3 sampler free.

Scholastic

2931 E. McCarty St.
Jefferson City, MO 65101
(800) 325-6149
(314) 635-5881 FAX

Educational books, children's paperbacks, supplemental materials, and teacher resources for grades K–8. Free catalog upon request. Inform Scholastic that you are home schooling to get specific information on placing orders.

Science Weekly

P.O. Box 70638
Chevy Chase, MD 20813-0638
(301) 680-8804
(800) 4WEEKLY
(301) 680-9240 FAX

Subscriptions available for activity-based science publications for seven different reading levels (K–8). Sixteen publications per year.

Shekinah Curriculum Cellar

967 Junipero Dr.
Costa Mesa, CA 92626
(714) 751-7767
(714) 751-7725 FAX

Large selection of Christian books and selected secular materials for home educators. Catalog available for $1.

Steck-Vaughn

P.O. Box 26015
Austin, TX 78755
(800) 531-5015
(512) 343-6854 FAX

Educational materials for elementary, secondary, adult, and special education. Materials for all major subject areas. Free catalog.

The Sycamore Tree, Inc.
Educational Services
2179 Meyer Place
Costa Mesa, CA 92627
(714) 650-4466 Information
(800) 779-6750 Ordering
http://www.Sycamoretree.com

Full-line catalog of home-school products plus a complete home-school program. Free catalog if you mention this resource book.

TOPS Learning Systems
10970 S. Mulino Road
Canby, OR 97013
(503) 263-2040
(503) 266-5200 FAX

Investigative science and problem-solving activities using everyday items.

V. J. Mortensen Co.
P.O. Box 98
Hayden, ID 83835-0098
(208) 664-6333
(800) 265-MATH for the West Coast
(800) 632-MATH for the Midwest and East Coast

Math manipulatives, workbooks, manuals, videos, and software. Chemistry workbooks (grades 4 and up).

Western Educational Activities
10929 101st St.
Edmonton, Alberta T5H 2S7
(403) 429-1086
(403) 426-5102 FAX

Distributors of supplementary materials of all kinds. Free catalog.

Window Tree Learning Project
12563 Carrs Landing Road
Winfield, British Columbia V4V 1A1
(604) 766-0568
(604) 766-4051 FAX

A variety of texts, workbooks, and resources (including Canadian history and geography) as well as workshops and assessments.

Zaner-Bloser Educational Publishers
2200 West Fifth Ave.
P.O. Box 16764
Columbus, OH 43216-6764
(614) 486-0221
(800) 421-3018
(614) 487-2699 FAX

Spelling and handwriting programs for K–8. Free catalog.

Zephyr Press
P.O. Box 66006
Tucson, AZ 85728-6006
(520) 322-5090
(520) 323-9402 FAX

Supplemental, research-based educational books, games, and materials with a holistic approach, incorporating multiple intelligences and individual learning styles.

Government Agencies

Write or call government agencies to obtain the most current legal requirements or guidelines, if any, for home education in your state, province, or territory. (All addresses and phone numbers were current at time of publication.)

UNITED STATES

ALABAMA
Coordinator-Accreditations
Gordon Persons Bldg.
50 N. Ripley
Montgomery, AL 36130-3901
(205) 242-8165

ALASKA
State Office Information
Education Administrator
Centralized Correspondence Study
Department of Education
P.O. Box GA
Juneau, AK 99811-0544
(907) 465-2835

ARIZONA
Director of Testing and Evaluation
Arizona Department of Education
1535 W. Jefferson St.
Phoenix, AZ 85007
(602) 542-3759

ARKANSAS
Program Manager
Arkansas Department of Education
4 Capitol Mall, Room 404 A
Little Rock, AR 72201
(501) 682-4233

CALIFORNIA
Deputy General Counsel
California Department of Education
P.O. Box 944272
Sacramento, CA 94244-2720
(916) 657-2453

COLORADO
State Office of Education
201 E. Colfax Ave.
Denver, CO 80203
(303) 866-6678

CONNECTICUT
School Approval Consultant
State Department of Education
P.O. Box 2219, Room 363
Hartford, CT 06145
(203) 566-3593

DELAWARE
Department of Public Instruction
P.O. Box 1402
Dover, DE 19903-1402
(302) 739-4583

DISTRICT OF COLUMBIA
D.C. Public Schools
Logan Administrative Building
215 G. Street N.E.
Washington, D.C. 20002
(202) 724-2397

FLORIDA
Program Specialist, Student Services
Florida Department of Education
Florida Education Center
325 West Gaines St.
Tallahassee, FL 32399
(904) 487-8567

GEORGIA
Georgia Department of Education
1662 Twin Towers E
Atlanta, GA 30334
(404) 656-2446

HAWAII
Student Personnel Services
2530 10th Ave., Bldg. A
Honolulu, HI 96816
(808) 733-9109

IDAHO
Department of Education
P.O. Box 83720
Boise, ID 83720-0027
(208) 334-2165

ILLINOIS
State Board of Planning
Research and Education
School Approval Section
100 N. First St.
Springfield, IL 62777
(217) 782-2948

INDIANA
Indiana Department of Education
Student Services, Room 229, State
House
Indianapolis, IN 46204-2798
(317) 232-9111

IOWA
Department of Education Consultant
Iowa Department of Education
Grimes State Office Building
Des Moines, IA 50319-0146
(515) 281-5294

KANSAS
State Board of Education
120 S.E. 10th Ave.
Topeka, KS 66612-1182
(913) 296-4318

KENTUCKY
Planning and Government Relations
Kentucky Department of Education
500 Mero St.
Frankfort, KY 40601
(502) 564-3421

LOUISIANA
Department of Education
P.O. Box 94064
Baton Rouge, LA 70804
(504) 342-3473

MAINE
Department of Education
State House Station #23
Augusta, ME 04333
(207) 287-5800

MARYLAND
State Department of Education
Special Services
200 W. Baltimore St.
Baltimore, MD 21201-2595
(410) 767-0408

MASSACHUSETTS
Massachusetts H.O.P.E.
15 Ohio St.
Wilmington, MA 01887
(508) 658-8970

MICHIGAN
Department of Education
P.O. Box 30008
Lansing, MI 48909
(517) 373-0796

MINNESOTA
Government Relations
Minnesota Department of Education
Room 710, Capitol Square Building
550 Cedar St.
St. Paul, MN 55101
(612) 296-6595

MISSISSIPPI
State Department of Education
Office of Community and Outreach
Services
723 N. Presidents St.
Jackson, MS 39201
(601) 359-3598

MISSOURI
Department of Elementary and
Secondary Education
P.O. Box 480
Jefferson City, MO 65102
(314) 751-7602

MONTANA
Office of Public Instruction
P.O. Box 202501
State Capitol
Helena, MT 59620-2501
(406) 444-4402

NEBRASKA
State Department of Education
301 Centennial Mall South
P.O. Box 94987
Lincoln, NE 68509-4987
(402) 471-2784

NEVADA
Nevada State Department of Education
Elementary and Secondary Education
Capitol Complex
400 West King St.
Carson City, NV 89710
(702) 687-3136

NEW HAMPSHIRE
State Department of Education
Division of Standards and Certification
101 Pleasant St.
Concord, NH 03301
(603) 271-3741

NEW JERSEY
New Jersey Department of Education
225 East State St.
CN 500
Trenton, NJ 08625
(609) 984-7814

NEW MEXICO
Management Support and Intervention
Unit
300 Dongasper
Sante Fe, NM 87501-2786
(505) 827-6588

NEW YORK
State Education Department
Room 471-EBA
Albany, NY 12234
(518) 474-3879

NORTH CAROLINA
Division of NonPublic Education
116 W. Jones St.
Raleigh, NC 27603-8001
(919) 733-4276

NORTH DAKOTA
Department of Public Instruction
State Capitol
600 East Boulevard Ave.
Bismark, ND 58505-0440
(701) 328-2295

OHIO
Department of Education
65 S. Front Street, Room 1009
Columbus, OH 43215
(614) 466-3304

OKLAHOMA
Department of Education
2500 N. Lincoln
Oklahoma City, OK 73105
(405) 521-3333

OREGON
State Department of Education
255 Capitol NE
Salem, OR 97310
(503) 378-5585, ex. 682

PENNSYLVANIA
Office of School Services
Department of Education
333 Market St.
Harrisburg, PA 17126-0333
(717) 783-3750

RHODE ISLAND
Commissioner of Education
Office of Legal Counsel
Department of Education
22 Hayes St.
Providence, RI 02908
(401) 277-2031, ext. 2500

SOUTH CAROLINA
Department of Education
1429 Senate St.
Columbia, SC 29201
(803) 734-8815

SOUTH DAKOTA
State Department of Education
Education Accountability
700 Governors Dr.
Pierre, SD 57501-2293
(605) 773-4770

TENNESSEE
School Approval, Home Schools, and
Private Schools
Gate Plaza, 710 James Robertson
Parkway
Nashville, TN 37243-8375
(615) 532-4711

TEXAS
Texas Education Agency
1701 N. Congress
Austin, TX 78701-1494
(512) 463-9354

UTAH
State Office of Education
250 E. 500 S.
Salt Lake City, UT 84111
(801) 538-7743

VERMONT
Home Study and Independent School
Consultant
Vermont Department of Education
School Improvement Unit
120 State St.
Montpelier, VT 05620
(802) 828-2756

VIRGINIA
Virginia Department of Education
Division of Compliance Coordination
P.O. Box 2120
Richmond, VA 23216-2120
(804) 225-2747

WASHINGTON
Superintendent of Public Instruction
P.O. Box 47200
Olympia, WA 98504-7200
(206) 753-6757

WEST VIRGINIA
State Coordinator of Home Schooling
West Virginia Department of Education
Office of Accreditation and
Recognition
Room 330, Bldg. 6, Capitol Complex
1900 Canawah Blvd. East
Charleston, WV 25305-0330
(304) 558-3788

WISCONSIN
Director, Bureau for School
Management Services and Federal Aid
State of Wisconsin, Department of
Public Instruction
125 S. Webster St.
P.O. Box 7841
Madison, WI 53707-7841
(608) 266-5761

WYOMING

Wyoming State Department of
Education
Hathaway Building, 2nd Floor
2300 Capitol Ave.
Cheyenne, WY 82002-0050
(307) 777-6268

CANADA

ALBERTA

Department of Education
Private School Coordinator
West Tower, Devonian Building
11160 Jasper Ave.
Edmonton, Alberta T5K OL2
(403) 427-7219
(403) 427-0591 FAX

BRITISH COLUMBIA

Ministry of Education
Independent Schools Branch
Parliament Buildings
Victoria, British Columbia V8V 2M4
(604) 356-0432
(604) 387-9695 FAX

MANITOBA

Department of Education and Training
Home School Coordinator
555 Main St.
Winkler, Manitoba R6W 1C4
(204) 325-2309
(800) 465-9915
(204) 325-4212 FAX

NEW BRUNSWICK

Department of Education
P.O. Box 6000
Fredericton, New Brunswick E38 5H1
(506) 453-3678
(506) 453-3325 FAX

NEWFOUNDLAND

Department of Education and Training
Government of Newfoundland and
Labrador
Confederation Building, West Block
Box 8700
St. John's, Newfoundland A1B 4J6
(709) 729-5097
(709) 729-5896 FAX

NORTHWEST TERRITORIES

Department of Education
Culture and Employment
Educational Development
P.O. Box 1320
Yellowknife, Northwest Territories
X1A 2L9
(403) 920-8061
(403) 873-0155 FAX

NOVA SCOTIA

Department of Education
Box 578
Halifax, Nova Scotia B3J 2S9
(902) 424-5829
(902) 424-0519 FAX

ONTARIO

Ministry of Education and Training
Provincial School Attendance
Counselor
10th Floor
Mowat Block, 900 Bay St.
Toronto, Ontario M7A 1L2
(416) 325-2224
(416) 325-2552 FAX

PRINCE EDWARD ISLAND

Department of Education
Box 2000
Charlottetown, Prince Edward Island
C1A 7N8
(902) 368-4600
(902) 368-4663 FAX

QUÉBEC

Ministère de l'Éducation
1035, Rue De La Chevrotière
Québec, Québec G1R 5A5
(418) 643-7095
(418) 646-6561 FAX

SASKATCHEWAN

Department of Education, Training and
Employment
Independent Schools and Home-Based
Education
3085 Albert St.
Regina, Saskatchewan S4P 3V7
(306) 787-7054
(306) 787-6139 FAX

YUKON TERRITORY

Department of Education
Government of the Yukon Territory
P.O. Box 2703
Whitehorse, Yukon Territory Y1A 2C6
(403) 667-5607
(403) 667-6339 FAX

Support Groups

This list of support groups is a starting point in locating organizations that will assist your family. Home schoolers in your area may have additional curriculum resource recommendations. (Addresses and telephone numbers were current at time of printing.)

Alliance for Parental Involvement in Education
P.O. Box 59
East Chatham, NY 12060-0059
(518) 392-6900

The Canadian Alliance of Homeschoolers
R.R. #1
St. George, Ontario N0E 1N0
(519) 448-4001

Canadian Home Educators' Association
S.S. #2, S-5, C-5
Kamloops, British Columbia V2C 6C3
(604) 374-6070 Phone and FAX

Christian Home Educators' Association
P.O. Box 2009
Norwalk, CA 90651-2009
(800) 564-CHEA general information
(310) 864-2432 information regarding specific states

Home Education League of Parents
3208 Cahuenga Boulevard West
Suite 131
Los Angeles, CA 90068
(800) 582-9061

Jewish Home Educators' Network and Newsletter
P.O. Box 300
Benton City, WA 99329
(509) 588-5013

Moore Foundation
Box 1
Camas, WA 98607
(206) 835-2736

National Challenged Homeschoolers' Association
Tom and Sherry Bushnell
5383 Alpine Road SE
Olalla, WA 98359
(206) 857-4257

Testing Materials

STANDARDIZED TESTS

Bob Jones University Press
Greenville, SC 29614
(800) 845-5731

Tests Provided:
1. Iowa Test of Basic Skills

2. Combined Iowa Achievement Test and Learning Cognitive Abilities Test

3. Tests of Achievement and Proficiency (high school)

4. Stanford Achievement Test (SAT)

Additional Information:
In order to administer the first three tests, Bob Jones requires that you be either:

• Currently certified as a teacher by a national or state organization

• A graduate of a four-year program

• A current teacher in an operating "conventional school"

These requirements were established in conjunction with Riverside Publishing Company, the test provider. For test security reasons, the test can only be mailed to the qualified tester and all testing materials, including answer sheets, must be returned within 50 days of receipt to Bob Jones University for scoring and interpretation. You get back an analysis of the results in five to seven weeks. Call for more details on the Stanford Achievement Test.

Canadian Test Centre
85 Citizen Court, Suite 7
Markham, Ontario L6G 1A8
(905) 513-6636
(800) 668-1006
(915) 513-6639 FAX

Tests Provided:
1. Canadian Achievement Test (CAT)
2. Canadian Test of Cognitive Skills

Nelson Canada
1120 Birchmount Road
Scarborough, Ontario M1K 5G4
(800) 268-2222, ext. 444
(416) 752-9100, ext. 444 Toronto
(416) 752-8101 FAX

Tests Provided:
1. Canadian Test of Basic Skills (CTBS)
2. Canadian Cognitive Abilities Test (CCAT)

TEST PREPARATION MATERIALS

Continental Press
520 E. Bainbridge St.
Elizabethtown, PA 17022
(800) 233-0759 United States
(717) 367-1836 Canada

Materials: On Target for Tests
Book A: (grades 2–3)
Book B: (grades 4–6)
Book C: (grades 7–9)

How to order: Many teacher supply stores and home-school suppliers carry these materials or you can order directly from Continental Press.

S.R.A., a division of McGraw-Hill
P.O. Box 543
Blacklick, Ohio 43004
(800) 442-9685 Canada
(800) 843-8855 U.S.A.
(614) 860-1877 U.S.A.

Materials: Scoring High
Book A: (grades 1–3)
Book B: (grades 3–5)
Book C: (grades 5–8)

How to order: Many home-school suppliers and teacher supply stores carry these materials, or you can order directly through S.R.A.

Commercial Learning Games

READING, SPELLING, VOCABULARY

Boggle®
Palabra®
Password
Rack-O®
Scrabble®
Up-Words®
Word Yahtzee

MEMORY

Memory®
Simon®
Vanished!®

MATH

Backgammon®
Dominoes
Don't Go to Jail®
Down & Out®
Greed®
Monopoly®
Stun®
24 Game™
Upbid™
Yahtzee®

THINKING STRATEGIES

Abalone®
The Amazing Labyrinth
Battleship®
Cathedral®
Checkers
Chess
Chinese Checkers
Clue®
Connect Four®
Eclipse™
5ive Straight®
Guess Who®
Imagic
Mage Stones™
Mankala
Mastermind®
No Dice™
Othello®
Pente ®
Risk ®
Shuttles®
Stratego®
Tangoes®
Traverse®

COOPERATION

Deep Sea Diver
Max
Mountaineering
Princess
Sky Travelers
Sleeping Grump

Bibliography

This bibliography is a list of books and magazines about home education and related topics. It has informative, useful readings and reference materials for parents getting started in home education. It is also helpful for veteran home educators wanting to sample a variety of materials on the subject.

BOOKS

Armstrong, Thomas. *In Their Own Way.* Jeremy P. Tarcher, Inc., 1987. A description of the distinct learning styles of children.

Colfax, David and Micki. *Homeschooling for Excellence.* Warner Books, 1988. The story of a family's 20 years of home-schooling experience.

Estell, Doug, Michele L. Satchwell, and Patricia S. Wright. *Reading Lists for College-Bound Students.* Prentice Hall, 1993. Annotated lists of the 100 books most often recommended by leading colleges and universities.

Gardner, Howard. *Multiple Intelligences: The Theory in Practice.* HarperCollins, 1993. A detailed explanation of the theory of multiple intelligences.

Gatto, John Taylor. *Dumbing Us Down: The Hidden Curriculum of Compulsory Schooling.* New Society Publishers, 1992. The New York Teacher of the Year addresses what he considers to be "the deadening heart" of compulsory schooling.

Guterson, David. *Family Matters: Why Homeschooling Makes Sense.* Harcourt Brace Jovanovich, 1992. A well-written and thoughtful discussion of current home-schooling issues and practices.

Healy, Janet M. *Endangered Minds.* Simon & Schuster, 1990. Examines the impact our educational system has on the intellectual development of children.

Holt, John. *Learning All the Time.* Addison-Wesley, 1989. John Holt was a respected educator and longtime critic of our educational system. Despairing of successful educational reform, he turned to home education as a solution. Along with the Raymond and Dorothy Moore, founders of the home-education movement, Holt advocated home education long before it was popular.

————. *Teach Your Own.* Delta, 1988. Advice and practical ideas about home education with an emphasis on interest-driven approaches.

Keirsey, David, and Marilyn Bates. *Please Understand Me.* Prometheus Nemesis Books, 1984. An introduction to temperament styles.

Markova, Dawna. *How Your Child Is Smart.* Conari Press, 1992. A discussion of modality-based learning patterns.

Moore, Raymond and Dorothy. *Home Grown Kids: A Practical Handbook for Teaching Your Children at Home.* Word Books, 1981. Tips for home schooling.

————. *School Can Wait: The Natural Child the First Eight Years.* Brigham Young University Press, 1979. Although Raymond Moore did not originate home schooling, he and his wife have been instrumental in launching the home-schooling movement in the 1980s. They are pioneers in contemporary home education and this book presents much of their philosophy.

————. *The Successful Home-School Family Handbook: A Creative and Stress-free Approach to Home Schooling.* Thomas Nelson, 1994. Helpful information for creating a successful home-school environment.

O'Leary, Jenifer. *Write Your Own Curriculum.* Whole Life Publishing, 1993. Assistance in planning, organizing, and documenting home-education curriculum.

Pedersen, Anne and Peggy O'Mara (editors). *Schooling at Home: Parents, Kids, and Learning.* John Muir Publications, 1990. A collection of essays on learning, legal issues, philosophy, methods, and personal accounts by the editors of *Mothering Magazine.*

Pride, Mary. *The Big Book of Home Learning.* Crossway Books, 1991. Four volumes of extensive coverage of materials, resources, and approaches to home education: *Getting Started, Preschool and Elementary, Teen and Adult, Afterschooling Extras.*

Smith, Frank. *Joining the Literacy Club.* Heinemann, 1988. Essays about how children learn to read and think. Although this book does not address home education, the information is pertinent to home-education parents.

Tobias, Cynthia. *The Way They Learn.* Focus on the Family, 1994. How to discover and teach to your child's strengths.

Trelease, Jim. *Read-Aloud Handbook for Parents.* Penguin, 1985. The value of oral reading, how to read aloud to your children, and recommended literature by age level.

Unger, Harlow G. *But What If I Don't Want to Go to College?* Facts On File, 1992. A guide to careers through alternative education.

Van Galen, Jane and Mary Anne Pitman, (editors). *Home Schooling: Political, Historical, and Pedagogical Perspectives.* Ablex Publishing Corporation, 1991. A scholarly look at the home-education movement.

HOME-EDUCATION PERIODICALS

Growing without Schooling. Holt Associates. 2269 Massachusetts Ave., Cambridge, MA 02140. Articles written about and by home-schooling parents and children with an emphasis on interest-driven education.

Home Education Magazine. Home Education Press. P.O. Box 1083, Tonasket, Washington 98855. (509) 486-1351. An informative bi-monthly magazine.

Home Education News. Box 39009, Point Grey RPO, Vancouver, British Columbia V6R 4P1. (604) 228-1939. Ten publications per year. All articles written by educators and parents who are currently home schooling.

Home School Researcher. National Home Education Research Institute c/o Western Baptist College. 5000 Deer Park Drive, S.E. Salem, Oregon 97301. (503) 581-8600. A quarterly publication of information and current research relevant to home education.

Natural Life. Wendy Pricsnitz (editor). RR #1, St. George, Ontario. N0E 1N0. Phone and FAX: (519) 448-4001. Monthly newspaper covering healthy eating habits, wellness, organic gardening, the environment, holistic parenting, home-based businesses, and home education.

Practical Homeschooling. Home Life, P.O. Box 1250, Fenton, MO 63026-1850. (800) 346-6322. A variety of articles, home-study helps, and advertisements, plus computer software information.

Quest—The Canadian Home Educator's Digest. 12128 95A St. N.W., Edmonton, Alberta T5G 1R9. FAX: (403) 293-4447. A Christian journal with national coverage.

Teaching Home. P.O. Box 20219, Portland, OR 97220-0219. (503) 253-9633. A Christian home-schooling magazine.

Glossary

Affidavit–formal notification filed with state or province officials of a parent's intent to operate a private school. Not all states or provinces require such affidavits.

Course of study–broad overview of topics and subject matter to be covered at a specific grade level.

Cumulative records–confidential records initiated when a student enrolls in kindergarten. These records usually include health information, test scores, report cards, and anecdotal notes recorded by the teacher. The cumulative record follows the student from grade to grade through high school.

Curriculum–the organized ideas, facts, and skills that make up a course of study.

Developing readers–students who have control over many early reading skills and have gained enough confidence in their abilities to take risks with unfamiliar material.

Diagnostic tests–tests used to provide information regarding a child's individual academic strengths and weaknesses.

Emergent readers–children who are starting to learn that a book tells a story. Children at this stage love being read to and ask to hear the same book again and again.

Extrinsic motivation–motivation that is external, such as praise, reward, or punishment. Extrinsic motivation might be receiving a reward or having a privilege taken away to reinforce or establish a behavior.]

Home school/home education–teaching a child at home. Instruction is usually provided by a parent or other family members. The terms, *home schooling* and *home education,* are often used interchangeably; however, some home educators make a distinction. They use home schooling to mean *school-like* in setting and approach. Home education connotes a broader outlook on learning and encompasses a wider variety of methods and goals.

Home-school cooperative–a group of home-school families who provide support for one another. Groups vary as to services provided. Most provide social opportunities as well as group classes and unit study activities.

Independent readers–students who are able to read unassisted at the appropriate level.

Independent Study Program (ISP)–a program established by a private or public school district that allows some students to complete their work off campus. Lesson plans and samples of completed work are usually submitted to school personnel for review and approval.

Intrinsic motivation–internal motivation; actions are based on the personal satisfaction of the activity or the results the activity will bring to the individual involved.

Learning styles–individual differences and preferences in focusing attention and acquiring, processing, and evaluating information. Learning styles encompass temperament and personality differences and acknowledge children's strengths and weaknesses. The closer the match between a child's learning style and the instructional approach, the easier and more rewarding the learning experience will be.

Locus of control–where responsibility for learning is placed.

Long-term planning–planning that is done prior to initial instruction. This planning highlights major skills, topics, and units to be covered in a given year.

Socialization–training a child for interaction in a social environment, including the ability to adapt to social needs. Socialization includes the abilities to participate actively in a group, to relate to others, and to form cooperative and interdependent relationships of a positive nature.

Standardized tests–tests that assess how a child performs in relationship to other children the same age, taking the same test, following the same guidelines. Scores are presented by a percentile ranking and/or a grade-level equivalent.

Student-directed learning–a setting in which course topics, curriculum materials, activities, and scheduling are primarily determined and selected by the students. The assumption is that the students as active learners know

what is most interesting and meaningful to them. They will learn more easily when they are studying material of interest.

Teacher-directed learning–a setting in which course topics, curriculum materials, activities, and scheduling are primarily determined and selected by the teacher. The assumption is that the teacher as an experienced adult knows what is best for the student.

Textbook-driven approach–an approach to home schooling that uses textbook lesson plans to organize the course of study.

Theme-driven approach–an approach to home schooling that uses specific concepts or units around which to organize the course of study.

Umbrella group–a private organization that offers to maintain the records of home-school students. Umbrella groups provide varying services to families which may include support, inservices, and counsel. A fee is usually charged. Some private schools and correspondence schools function as umbrella groups.

Weekly assignment sheets/lesson plans–teaching plans or records listing concepts to be taught in a given week. Plans usually include a concept and how that concept will be presented.

Whole language–an approach to teaching reading and writing where skills are taught in the natural context of language rather than in isolation.